ECONOMIC ISSUES, PROBLEMS AND PERSPECTIVES

CAPITAL GAINS TAXATION

EFFECTS AND PROPOSALS

ECONOMIC ISSUES, PROBLEMS AND PERSPECTIVES

Additional books in this series can be found on Nova's website under the Series tab.

Additional E-books in this series can be found on Nova's website under the E-book tab.

MONETARY, FISCAL AND TRADE POLICIES

Additional books in this series can be found on Nova's website under the Series tab.

Additional E-books in this series can be found on Nova's website under the E-book tab.

ECONOMIC ISSUES, PROBLEMS AND PERSPECTIVES

CAPITAL GAINS TAXATION

EFFECTS AND PROPOSALS

MATT T. ZIMMERMAN
AND
LYLE L. CURTIS
EDITORS

Nova Science Publishers, Inc.
New York

Library of Congress Cataloging-in-Publication Data

ISBN 978-1-62081-076-7

Published by Nova Science Publishers, Inc. † New York

CONTENTS

Preface		**vii**
Chapter 1	Capital Gains Taxes: An Overview *Jane G. Gravelle*	**1**
Chapter 2	The Economic Effects of Capital Gains Taxation *Thomas L. Hungerford*	**11**
Chapter 3	Capital Gains Tax Options: Behavioral Responses and Revenues *Jane G. Gravelle*	**27**
Chapter 4	Tax Treatment of Long-Term Capital Gains and Dividends and Related Provisions in the President's FY2011 Budget Proposal *Maxim Shvedov*	**53**
Index		**75**

PREFACE

This book examines the effects and proposals of capital gains taxation. Tax legislation in 1997 reduced capital gains taxes on several types of assets, imposing a 20% maximum tax rate on long-term gains, a rate temporarily reduced to 15% for 2003-2008, which was extended for two additional years in 2006. There is also an exclusion of $500,000 ($250,000 for single returns) for gains on home sales. Some believe that lower capital gains taxes will cost little compared to the benefits they bring and that lower taxes induce additional economic growth, although the magnitude of these potential effects is in some dispute. Others criticize lower capital gains taxes as benefiting higher income individuals and express concerns about the budget effects, particularly in future years.

Pending expiration at the end of 2010 of tax cuts enacted during the presidency of George W. Bush raises important questions about the future of affected tax policies. Tax treatment of longterm capital gains and dividends was one of the key components of the overall tax cut package. Long-term capital gains or losses arise from a sale or exchange of a capital asset, such as shares of stock, held for a year or longer by a taxpayer. Dividends are any distributions made by a corporation to its shareholders. This report discusses their tax treatment under current law and the President's FY2011 Budget Proposal, analyzes economic characteristics of affected taxpayers, and presents some policy alternatives with respect to this element of the tax system.

Historically capital gains and dividends were often treated differently from ordinary income, such as salaries and wages, and from each other. With the passage of the Jobs and Growth Tax Relief Reconciliation Act of 2003 (JGTRRA, P.L. 108-27), long-term capital gains and qualified dividends were taxed at identical rates. In 2010 the rates are 15% or 0%, the latter if a taxpayer's marginal tax rate on ordinary income is 15% or lower. This treatment compares to the tax rates of 10% to 35% on ordinary income in 2010 (changing to 15% to 39.6% in 2011 under current law). If tax reductions first enacted under JGTRRA are allowed to expire, long-term capital gains would become subject to 20% or 10% rate and dividends would be treated as ordinary income and subject to ordinary tax rates.

In: Capital Gains Taxation
Editors: M. Zimmerman, L. Curtis
ISBN: 978-1-62081-076-7

Chapter 1

CAPITAL GAINS TAXES: AN OVERVIEW*

Jane G. Gravelle

SUMMARY

Tax legislation in 1997 reduced capital gains taxes on several types of assets, imposing a 20% maximum tax rate on long-term gains, a rate temporarily reduced to 15% for 2003-2008, which was extended for two additional years in 2006. Legislation enacted in December 2010 extended the lower rates for an additional two years, thorough 2010.There is also an exclusion of $500,000 ($250,000 for single returns) for gains on home sales. The capital gains tax has been a tax cut target since the 1986 Tax Reform Act treated capital gains as ordinary income. An argument for lower capital gains taxes is reduction of the lock-in effect. Some also believe that lower capital gains taxes will cost little compared to the benefits they bring and that lower taxes induce additional economic growth, although the magnitude of these potential effects is in some dispute. Others criticize lower capital gains taxes as benefitting higher income individuals and express concerns about the budget effects, particularly in future years. Another criticism of lower rates is the possible role of a larger capital gains tax differential in encouraging tax sheltering activities and adding complexity to the tax law.

* This is an edited, reformatted and augmented version of Congressional Research Services publication 96-769, dated January 5, 2011.

WHAT ARE CAPITAL GAINS AND HOW ARE THEY TAXED?

Capital gain arises when an asset is sold and consists of the difference between the basis (normally the acquisition price) and the sales price. Corporate stock accounts for 20% to 80% of taxable gains, depending on stock market performance. Real estate is the remaining major source of capital gains, although gain also arises from other assets (e.g., timber sales and collectibles). The appreciation in value can be real or reflect inflation. Corporate stock appreciates both because the firm's assets increase with reinvested earnings and because general price levels are rising. Appreciation in the value of property may simply reflect inflation. For depreciable assets, some of the gain may reflect the possibility that the property was depreciated too quickly.

If the return to capital gains were to be effectively taxed at the statutory tax rate in the manner of other income, real gains would have to be taxed in the year they accrue. Current practice departs from this approach. Gains are not taxed until realized, benefitting from the deferral of taxes. (Taxes on interest income are due as the interest is accrued.) Gains on an asset held until death may be passed on to heirs with the tax forgiven; if the asset is then sold, the gain is sales price less market value at the time of death, a treatment referred to as a "step-up in basis."

Under current law, there is a maximum tax of 20% on capital gains held for a year (temporarily reduced to 15% for 2003-2012), although the ordinary income tax rates reach as high as 39.6% (temporarily reduced to 35%). Where ordinary tax rates are 15% or below, the capital gains tax is 10% (temporarily at 5% for 2003-2007 and 0% for 2008-2012). Assuming the temporary provisions expire, gain from assets held five years and acquired after 2000 will be subject to a maximum rate of 18%. For gains in the 15% bracket and below, an 8% rate will apply to any gain on assets held for five years and sold after 2000, with no required acquisition date. Gain arising from prior depreciation deductions is taxed at ordinary rates, but there is a 25% ceiling rate on the gain from attributable to prior straight-line depreciation on real property. Gain from collectibles is taxed at 28%.

Under law prior to 1997, several rules permitted avoidance or deferral of the tax on gain on owner-occupied housing, including a provision allowing deferral of gain until a subsequent house is sold (rollover treatment) and a provision allowing a one-time exclusion of $125,000 of gain for those 55 and over. These provisions were replaced with a general $500,000 exclusion ($250,000 for a single individual), which cost only slightly more in revenue.

In contrast to these provisions that benefit capital gains, capital gains are penalized because many of the gains that are subject to tax arise from inflation and therefore do not reflect real income.

A Brief History

Capital gains were taxed when the income tax (with rates up to 7%) was imposed in 1913. An alternative rate of 12.5% was allowed in 1921 (the regular top rate was 73%). Tax rates were cut several times during the 1920s. Capital gain exclusions based on holding period were enacted in 1924, and modified in 1938, to deal with bunching of gains in one year. In 1942 a 50% exclusion was adopted, with an alternative rate of 25%. Over time, the top rate on ordinary income varied, rising to 94% in the mid-1940s, then dropping to 70% after 1964. In 1969 a new minimum tax increased the gains tax for some; the 25% alternative tax was repealed.

In 1978 the minimum tax on capital gains was repealed and the exclusion increased to 60% with a maximum rate of 28% (0.4 times 0.7). The top rate on ordinary income was reduced to 50% in 1981, reducing the capital gains rate to 20% (0.4 times 0.5). The Tax Reform Act of 1986 reduced tax rates further, but, in order to maintain distributional neutrality, eliminated some tax preferences, including the exclusion for capital gains. This treatment brought the rate for high income individuals in line with the rate on ordinary income—28%.

In 1989, President Bush proposed a top rate of 15%, halving top rates. The Ways and Means Committee considered two proposals: Chairman Rostenkowski proposed to index capital gains, and Representatives Jenkins, Flippo, and Archer proposed a 30% capital gains exclusion through 1991 followed by inflation indexation. This latter measure was approved by the Committee, but was not enacted.

In 1990, the President proposed a 30% exclusion, setting the rate at 19.6% for high income individuals. The House also passed a 50% exclusion with a lifetime maximum ceiling and a $1,000 annual exclusion, but this provision was not enacted into law. When rates on high income individuals were set at 31%, however, the capital gains rate was capped at 28%.

In 1991, the President again proposed a 30% exclusion, but no action was taken. In 1992, the President proposed a 45% exclusion. The House adopted a proposal for indexation for inflation for newly acquired assets: the Senate passed a separate set of graduated rates on capital gains that tended to benefit more moderate income individuals. This latter provision was included in a bill (H.R. 4210) containing many other tax provisions that was vetoed by the President.

No changes were proposed by President Clinton or adopted in 1993 and 1994 with the exception of a narrowly targeted benefit for small business stock adopted in 1993. The value of the tax cap was increased, however, in 1993 when new brackets of 36% and 39.6% were added for ordinary income.

In 1994, the "Contract With America" proposed a 50% exclusion for capital gains, and indexing the basis for all subsequent inflation, while eliminating the 28% cap; this exclusion would be about a 40% reduction on average from current rates. The Ways and Means Committee reported out H.R. 1215 which restricted inflation indexing to newly acquired assets (individuals could "mark to market"—pay tax on the difference between fair market value and basis as if the property were sold to qualify for indexation), did not allow indexation to create losses and provided a flat 25% tax rate for corporations). The 1995 reconciliation bill (H.R. 2491) that was vetoed by the President, included these revisions but delayed the indexation provision until 2002. During the 1996 presidential election, Mr. Dole proposed a slightly larger capital gains cut, and both candidates supported elimination of capital gains taxes on virtually all gains from home sales.

In 1997, the President and Congress agreed to a tax cut as part of the reconciliation. The Administration tax cut proposal included the change in tax treatment of owner occupied housing. The House bill included a reduction in the 15% and 28% rates to 10% and 20%, about a 30% cut. Capital gains would also be indexed for assets acquired after 2000 and held for three years; markto-market would also be allowed. The Senate and the final bill did not include indexing. The capital gains issue was briefly revisited in 1998, when the holding period for long term gains was moved back from the 18 months set in 1997 to the one year period that has typically applied. The 1999 House bill would have cut the rates to 15% and 10%: the conference version cut rates to 18% and 8% and proposed indexing of future gains, but the bill was vetoed. Capital gains were discussed during the consideration of the economic stimulus bill at the end of 2002, but not included in any legislative proposal (and no proposal was adopted). The temporary provisions for lower rates of 15% for 2003-2008 for those in the higher brackets and to 5% in 2003-2007 and 0% in 2008 for taxpayers in the 15% bracket or lower were adopted in 2003. H.R. 4297, adopted in 2006, extended these lower rates for two more years. P.L. 111-312, enacted in 2010, extended the lower rates for an additional two years, through 2010.

REVENUE EFFECTS

Over the past several years, a debate has ensued regarding the revenue cost of cutting capital gains taxes. For example, when the President proposed a 30% exclusion in 1990, Treasury estimates showed a $12 billion gain in revenue over the first five years, while the Joint Committee on Taxation found a revenue loss of approximately equal size.

Although the estimates seemed quite different, they both incorporated significant expected increases in the amount of gains realized as a result of the tax cut. For example, the Treasury would have estimated a revenue loss of $80 billion over five years with no behavioral response, and the Joint Tax Committee a loss of $100 billion. (The gap between these static estimates arose from differences in projections of expected capital gains, a volatile series that is quite difficult to estimate.)

Empirical evidence on capital gains realizations does not clearly point to a specific response and revenue cost. Recent research suggests long-run responses may be more modest than those suggested by the economics literature during the 1990 debate, but the short-run response is still difficult to ascertain. (For a survey of this literature, see Jane G. Gravelle, *The Economic Effects of Taxing Capital Income*, Cambridge, MA: MIT Press, 1984, pp. 143-151; see also Leonard Burman, *The Labyrinth of Capital Gains Tax Policy*, Washington, DC: The Brookings Institution, 1999, for a discussion of this issue and many others.) A review of recent developments in this literature is in CRS Report R41364, *Capital Gains Tax Options: Behavioral Responses and Revenues*, by Jane G. Gravelle.

Any revenue feedback effect will be smaller the larger the tax reduction. When the tax reduction is large, although there will be a larger response, any induced revenues will be taxed at the new lower rates. Thus, a 50% exclusion will not have as large a feedback effect relative to the static estimate as a 30% exclusion. Moreover, allowing a prospective tax cut that depends on selling and acquiring a new asset to qualify (or marking to market) as is the case for the reduction from 20% to 18% for five-year property causes a gain in the short run as well.

Arguments have also been made that a capital gains tax cut will induce additional savings, also resulting in a feedback effect as taxes are imposed on new income. This effect is uncertain, as it is not clear that an increase in the rate of return will increase savings (savings can decrease if the income effect is more powerful than the substitution effect) and what the magnitude of the response might be. (See Congressional Budget Office Memorandum, *An Analysis of the Potential Macroeconomic Effects of the Economic Growth Act of 1998*). There is also a debate about the effect of the capital gains tax on growth through its effect on innovation. Regardless of these empirical uncertainties, any effect of savings on taxable income in the short run is likely to be quite small due to the slow rate of capital accumulation. (Net savings are typically only about 2% to 3% of the capital stock, so that even a 10% increase in the savings rate would result in only a 2/10 to 3/10 of a percent first-year increase in the capital stock.) A related argument is that the tax cut will increase asset values; such an effect is only temporary, however, and will, if it occurs, only shift revenues from the future to the present. (For a discussion of savings and asset valuations, see testimony of Jane G. Gravelle, Congressional Research Service, before the Senate Finance Committee, February 15, 1995, and the House Ways and Means Committee, March 19, 1997.)

Impact on Effective Tax Burdens

The tax burden on an investment is influenced by both the tax rate and any benefits allowed or penalties imposed. One way to measure this tax burden is to calculate a marginal effective tax rate that captures in a single number all of the factors that affect tax burden. It is the percentage difference between the before- and after-tax return to investment, or the estimated statutory rate that would be applied to economic income to give the taxpayer the same burden as the combination of tax benefits and penalties.

The effective tax rate on capital gains can be either higher or lower than the statutory rate, depending on the inflation rate relative to the real appreciation rate and the holding period. Also, assets held until death are not subject to tax. For example, under prior law, assuming a 20% statutory tax rate, the gain on a growth stock (paying no dividends) with a real appreciation rate of 7% and an inflation rate of 3% would, if held for one year, seven years, 20 years, and until death, be subject respectively to tax rates of 27%, 22%, 14%, and 0%. The rate on 7- and 20-year assets would be 18%, for effective tax rates of 19% and 12%. (With no inflation and a 20% rate, the rates would be 19%, 16%, 12% and 0%; inflation penalizes assets held a shorter period more heavily than assets held for a longer period). Since less than half of gains that are accrued are realized, the effective tax rate is probably lower than the statutory tax rate. These benefits are larger for individuals who in the highest tax brackets (31%, 36%, and 39.6%) because the capital gains tax rate is capped at 20%. The rates would be lowered proportionally with a 15% tax rate.

Issues: Efficiency, Growth, Distribution, and Complexity

One argument in favor of reducing the capital gains tax is the lock-in effect. If this effect is large, the tax introduces significant distortions in behavior with relatively little revenue gain. Another way to reduce lock-in is accrual taxation (i.e., tax gains on a current basis as accrued), but this approach is only feasible when assets can be easily valued (e.g., publicly traded corporate stock). Another way to reduce lock-in is to tax gains passed on at death. These solutions may face technical problems and taxation of gains at death has been unpopular.

For owner-occupied housing, although there were many ways to avoid the tax under current law, the rules may have resulted in individuals remaining in houses that are too large if economic circumstances have declined (for example, through job loss or retirement or from a preference for a smaller home, or if there is relocation to a lower-cost area.)

A case might be made for lower capital gains taxes on corporate stock because corporate equity capital is subject to heavy taxation. This heavy taxation encourages corporations to take on too much debt and directs too much capital to the noncorporate sector. On the other hand, lower capital gains taxes increase the relative penalty that applies to dividends and introduce tax distortions in the decisions of the firm to retain earnings. This latter effect, however, does not occur under the temporary tax cuts that benefit dividends as well as capital gains.

Arguments have also been made that lower gains taxes will increase economic growth and entrepreneurship. Although evidence on the effect of tax cuts on savings rates and, thus, economic growth is difficult to obtain, most evidence does not indicate a large response of savings to an increase in the rate of return. Indeed, not all studies find a positive response, because a higher rate of return may allow individuals to save less while reaching their desired goal. (See Gravelle, *The Economics of Taxing Capital Income*, MIT Press, pp. 24-

28, for a survey.) A more effective route to increasing savings may be to take revenues that might otherwise finance a tax cut and reduce the debt.

Although arguments are made that lower gains taxes stimulate innovation and entrepreneurship, there is little evidence in history to connect periods of technical advance with lower taxes or even high rates of return. The extent to which entrepreneurs take tax considerations into account is unclear; however, there is some reason to doubt that capital gains taxes are important in obtaining large amounts of venture capital, in part because much of this capital is supplied by those not subject to the capital gains tax (i.e., pension funds, foreign investors). (See CRS Report RL30040, *Capital Gains Taxes, Innovation and Growth*, by Jane G. Gravelle, for a further discussion of capital gains taxes and venture capital.) Moreover, there is no evidence that longer corporate stock holding periods lead to more investments in long-term assets, including R&D, a rationale for lowering rates for assets with longer holding periods. (Note that indexing, initially proposed, and then dropped, favors assets with shorter holding periods.)

A major complaint made by some about lower gains rates cut is that they primarily benefit very high income individuals. Capital gains are concentrated among higher income individuals because these individuals tend to own capital and because they are likely to own capital that generates capital gains. For example, the Joint Committee on Taxation indicated that for 2005, 88% of the benefit of lower rates to individuals with incomes over $200,000 and 95% would go to individuals with incomes over $100,000. Individuals with $200,000 of income account for about 3% of taxpayers and individuals with incomes over $100,000 account for less about 14%. The distributional effects of the capital gains relief for homes is somewhat less concentrated at the higher end (although lower income individuals are much less likely to own homes). The revisions may also enhance horizontal equity by treating taxpayer in different circumstances more evenly.

Critics of lower capital gains taxes cite the contribution of preferential capital gains treatment to tax sheltering activities and complexity. For example, individuals may borrow (while deducting interest in full) to make investments that are eligible for lower capital gains tax rates, thereby earning high rates of return. These effects are, however, constrained in some cases (i.e., a passive loss restriction limits the deductions allowed in real estate ventures). Capital gains differentials complicate the tax law, especially as applied to depreciable assets where capital gains treatment can create incentives for churning assets unless recapture provisions are adopted. Indexing capital gains for inflation is more complicated than a simple exclusion, since different basis adjustments must apply to different vintages of assets and proper indexing of gains on depreciable property is especially difficult. Thus, foregoing indexing probably kept the tax law simpler.

In: Capital Gains Taxation
Editors: M. Zimmerman, L. Curtis
ISBN: 978-1-62081-076-7

Chapter 2

THE ECONOMIC EFFECTS OF CAPITAL GAINS TAXATION*

Thomas L. Hungerford

SUMMARY

One provision of the 1913 individual income tax that generated a great deal of confusion was the taxation of income from the sale of property (i.e., capital gains income). This initial confusion has led to almost 100 years of legislative debates over capital gains. Beginning in 1922 capital gains were first subject to lower tax rates than ordinary income. This preferential treatment has continued throughout most of the history of the income tax. Proposals dealing with the taxation of capital gains have ranged from the outright elimination of capital gains taxation to the reduction of capital gains tax rates for certain classes of taxpayers to the elimination of the preferential tax treatment.

Overall, capital gains tax revenues have been a fairly small, but not trivial, source of government revenue. Since 1954, revenue from the capital gains tax as a share of total income tax revenue has averaged 5.2%. It reached a peak of 12.8% in 1986 and a low of 2.0% in 1957. Nonetheless, the 2007 capital gains tax revenue of $123 billion was equal to 75% of the FY2007 budget deficit.

Some argue that reducing capital gains tax rates will increase tax revenues by dramatically increasing capital gains realizations. While the

* This is an edited, reformatted and augmented version of Congressional Research Services publication R40411, dated June 18, 2010.

effect of changes in the capital gains tax rate continue to be debated and researched, the bulk of the evidence suggests that reducing the capital gains tax rate reduces tax revenues.

Higher income households are substantially more likely to own assets that can generate taxable gains than lower income households. Additionally, high income households own most of these assets, realize most of the capital gains, and pay most of the capital gains taxes at preferential rates.

Capital gains tax reductions are often proposed as a policy that will increase saving and investment, provide a short-term economic stimulus, and boost long-term economic growth. Capital gains tax rate reductions appear to decrease public saving and may have little or no effect on private saving. Consequently, many analysts note that capital gains tax reductions likely have a negative overall impact on national saving. Furthermore, capital gains tax rate reductions, they observe, are unlikely to have much effect on the long-term level of output or the path to the long-run level of output (i.e., economic growth). A tax reduction on capital gains would mostly benefit very high income taxpayers who are likely to save most of any tax reduction. A temporary capital gains tax reduction possibly could have a negative impact on short-term economic growth.

INTRODUCTION

One provision of the 1913 individual income tax that generated a great deal of confusion was the taxation of income from the sale of property (i.e., capital gains income). This initial confusion has led to almost 100 years of legislative debates over capital gains. For the first nine years of the individual income tax, capital gains received no preferential treatment and were taxed as ordinary income. Beginning in 1922, however, capital gains were first subject to lower tax rates than ordinary income. This preferential treatment has continued throughout most of the history of the income tax.

Proposals and legislation dealing with the taxation of capital gains have ranged from the outright elimination of capital gains taxation to the reduction of capital gains tax rates for certain classes of taxpayers to the elimination of the preferential tax treatment. For example, the American Recovery and Reinvestment Act of 2009 (ARRA; P.L. 111-5) increased the exclusion of capital gains from the sale of certain small business stock held for more than five years from 50% to 75%.

HOW CAPITAL GAINS ARE TAXED

Proposals to deal with how capital gains are taxed depend on how capital gains are defined. Under the Haig-Simons approach, income is defined as consumption plus the change in wealth.[1] Wealth can increase because of active saving or because the value of assets has increased; capital gains are the increase in the value of capital assets. Under this income definition, real or inflation-adjusted capital gains would be taxed each year as they accrue and real capital losses would be deducted. It has long been recognized, however, that taxing real capital gains as they accrue may be impractical especially for capital assets that are not actively traded.

Given the difficulties of taxing capital gains as they accrue, capital gains are taxed as they are realized (that is, when the capital asset is sold or exchanged). Capital assets are property, but there are exceptions such as business inventory, accounts receivable acquired in the ordinary course of business, copyrights, and literary compositions.[2] Capital gains are calculated by subtracting the asset's basis from the sales price. An asset's basis is the original purchase price adjusted for certain additions and deductions; it is not adjusted for inflation. If the basis is greater than the sales price then it is a capital loss.

Capital gains are taxed at various rates. For the 2008 tax year, short-term capital gains (gains on capital assets held for less than one year) are taxed as ordinary income. Long-term capital gains are taxed at a 0% tax rate for taxpayers in the two lowest tax brackets (the 10% and 15% tax brackets) and at 15% for other taxpayers. Capital gains and capital losses are treated asymmetrically. Capital losses are subtracted from capital gains before calculating tax liability. If capital losses exceed capital gains, then up to $3,000 of capital losses can be deducted from ordinary income. Capital losses in excess of $3,000 can be carried over and subtracted from income in future years.[3]

CAPITAL GAINS TAX RATES AND TAX REVENUES

Both capital gains tax rates and tax revenues have constantly changed since the establishment of the income tax. Tax revenues depend on the tax rate and capital gains realizations. Capital gains realizations, in turn, depend on tax rates as well as other factors.

Tax Rates

Throughout most of the history of the income tax, the maximum capital gains tax rate has been lower than the maximum tax rate on ordinary income. Figure 1 displays the capital gains and ordinary income tax rates for the past 50 years. With the exception of a three-year period (1988- 1990), the capital gains tax rate was considerably below the tax rate for ordinary income. After 2010, the capital gains tax rate is scheduled to revert back to 20%. The 15% maximum capital gains tax rate between 2003 and 2010 is the lowest rate on long-term capital gains since the Second World War.

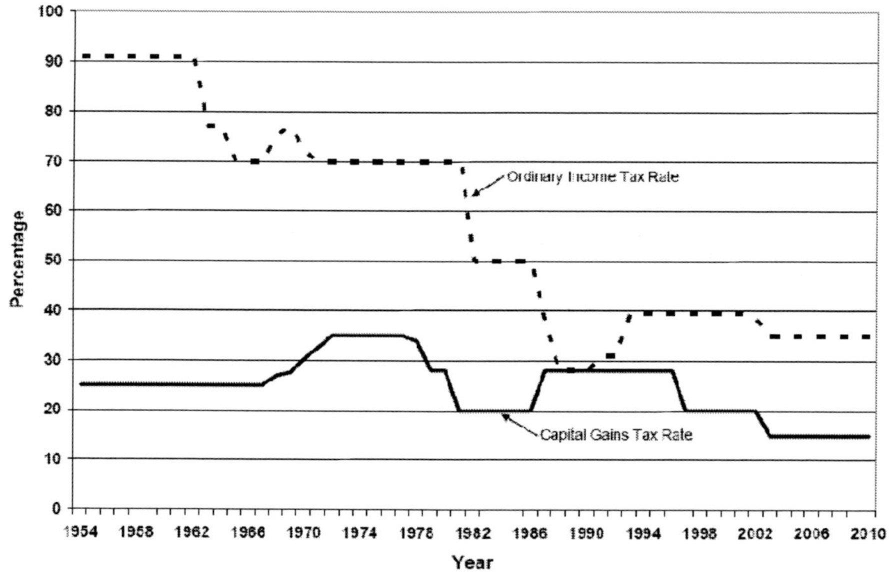

Source: Department of the Treasury.

Figure 1. Maximum Tax Rates on Capital Gains and Ordinary Income, 1954-2010.

Tax Revenues

Overall, capital gains tax revenues have been a fairly small, but not trivial, source of government revenue. Since 1954, revenue from the capital gains tax as a share of total income tax revenue has averaged 5.2%. It reached a peak of 12.8% in 1986 and a low of 2.0% in 1957. Nonetheless, the 2007 capital gains tax revenue of $123 billion was equal to 75% of the FY2007 budget deficit.

Capital gains tax revenue generally follows the same trend as capital gains realizations. Figure 2 shows both as a percentage of gross domestic product (GDP) from 1954 to 2008 along with CBO projections to 2019. Realizations and revenues hit peaks in 1986, 2000, and 2007.

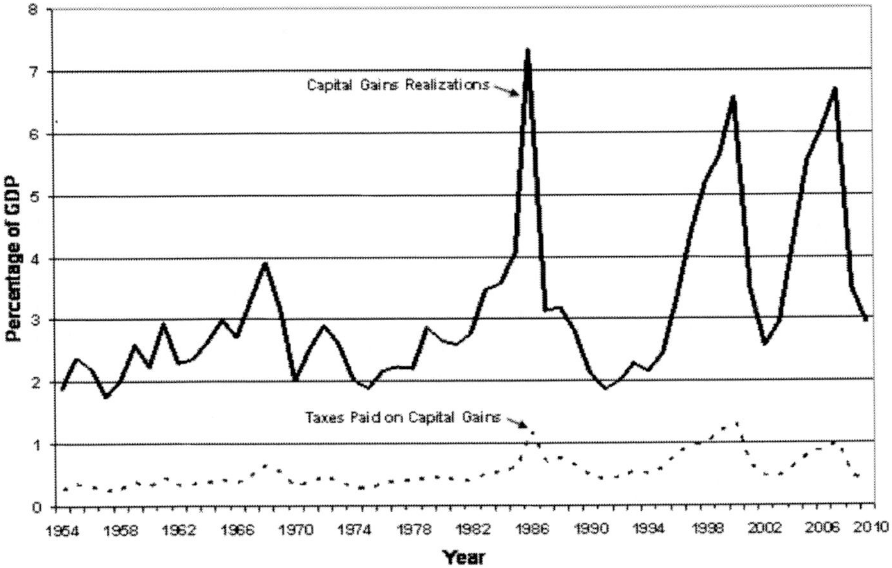

Figure 2. Capital Gains Realizations and Tax Revenue, 1954-2010; (As a percentage of GDP) Source: Department of the Treasury and CBO.

Behavioral Responses to Capital Gains Tax Rate Changes

The capital gains tax discourages capital gains realizations because capital gains are only taxed when realized. Consequently, taxpayers tend to hold on to appreciated assets they would otherwise sell. Furthermore, step-up in basis at death gives taxpayers an incentive to hold assets until death and pass them to their heirs. In these ways, the capital gains tax is said to produce a "lock-in" effect. This effect imposes efficiency losses because investors may be encouraged to hold suboptimal portfolios or forego investment opportunities with higher pre-tax returns. Changes in the capital gains tax rate can exacerbate or reduce lock-in effects, and thus affect realizations and tax revenues.

Changes in the capital gains tax rate tend to track capital gains realizations. Figure 3 shows the maximum capital gains tax rate and capital gains realizations as a percentage of GDP. The major spikes in realizations correspond to changes in the tax rate. The simple correlation between the two time-series is -0.64, which suggests that realizations increase when the tax rate decreases. It is this relationship that has led some to argue that decreasing the capital gains tax rate will increase capital gains tax revenues.

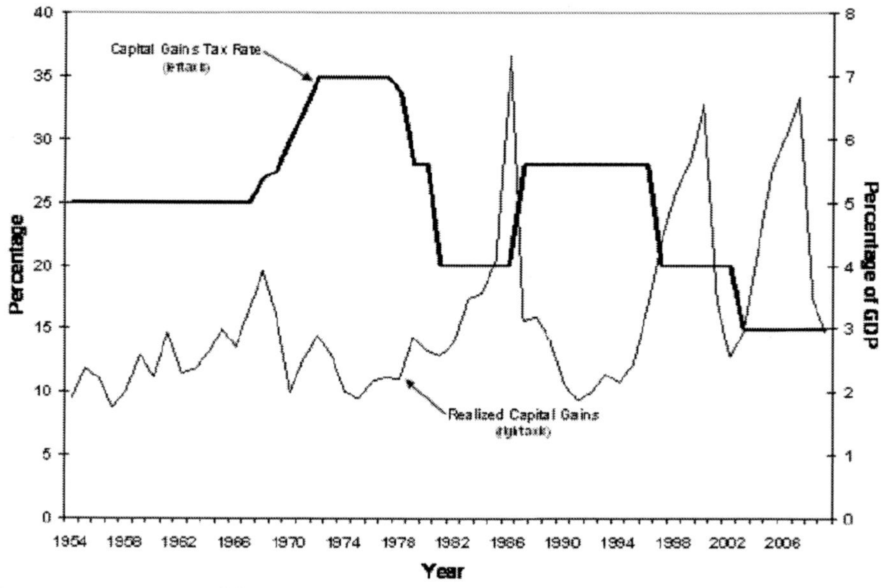

Source: Department of the Treasury.

Figure 3. Capital Gains Tax Rates and Realizations, 1954-2009.

An early study by Martin Feldstein, Joel Slemrod, and Shlomo Yitzhaki examined capital gains realizations and concluded that "reducing the tax on capital gains would not only encourage a more active market in corporate stock but would also increase tax revenue."[4] Their estimated elasticity was about 3.8, suggesting that a 10% reduction in the tax rate would increase realizations by 38%.

This estimate was criticized because it used data from only one year—1973.[5] This cross-sectional evidence was likely picking up a temporary timing response in realizations from the tax rate change rather than a behavioral response to a permanent change in the tax rate.[6]

Some analysts have argued that a large permanent response to capital gains tax rate changes is implausible. Alan Auerbach has suggested that there is nothing in the historical record of capital gains to justify a large elasticity.[7] Jane Gravelle points out that capital gains realizations cannot be greater than accruals. Her simulation model suggests an upper limit for the permanent realization elasticity is 0.5.[8]

Empirical research has tried to separate the transitory response from the permanent response. Gerald Auten and Charles Clotfelter used panel data, a dataset containing observations on individuals over a period of years (1969 to 1973), to estimate the temporary and permanent effects of a capital gains tax cut.[9]

They estimate a transitory elasticity that is generally greater than 1.0 (the simple average from all their specifications is 1.5) suggesting that a 10% reduction in the tax rate would lead to a 15% increase in short-run realizations (the timing response). The permanent or long-run elasticity they estimated was 0.5.

In subsequent research, Leonard Burman and William Randolph estimate a permanent elasticity that is closer to zero than to 0.5.[10] They, however, report a large transitory elasticity of 6.4. A large transitory elasticity and a low permanent elasticity are consistent with the pattern of capital gains realizations shown in Figure 3.

Changes in the tax rate or anticipated changes have coincided with large increases in capital gains realizations, but realizations quickly fell back to previous levels. The spike in 1986 was due to the transitory response to the announced increase in the capital gains tax rate to take effect in 1987. The spikes in 2000 and 2007 were the transitory responses to capital gains tax rate reductions.

Over the years, a variety of studies have estimated different long-run or permanent realizations elasticities. The general trend has been to estimate elasticities closer to zero than to 1.0 as data and estimation methods improve, though there are exceptions. However, even an elasticity of 1.0 does not mean that reducing the capital gains tax rate is revenue neutral. Taxpayers may increase their capital gains realizations by shifting other income into capital gains.

This may increase capital gains tax revenue, but will reduce tax revenues from other sources—overall, tax revenues fall. While the effect of changes in the capital gains tax rate continue to be debated and researched, the bulk of the evidence suggests that reducing the capital gains tax rate reduces tax revenues.

DISTRIBUTIONAL ISSUES

Three questions can be asked about distributional issues related to capital gains: (1) who owns the assets that can generate capital gains? (2) who realizes capital gains? and (3) who pays capital gains taxes? Each question is examined. Two data sources are used for the analysis: the Federal Reserve Board's 2007 Survey of Consumer Finances (SCF) and the IRS's 2004 Statistics of Income Public Use File (SOI PUF). See the Appendix for a description of each data source.

Assets and Accrued Capital Gains

Most assets owned by households would not be subject to capital gains taxes when sold. Figure 4 reports the various assets that households owned in 2007. Over half of the total is accounted for by retirement accounts (e.g., 401(k)s and IRAs) and principal residences. Retirement accounts generally are not taxed until the funds are withdrawn at retirement. At that time, the withdrawals are taxed as ordinary income. Up to $500,000 of the gain from the sale of a principal residence can be excluded from income taxes. Farm and business assets and other real estate (e.g., rental property, and vacation homes) account for 33% of household assets. The final 13% of household assets are financial assets (i.e., stocks, bonds, and mutual funds).

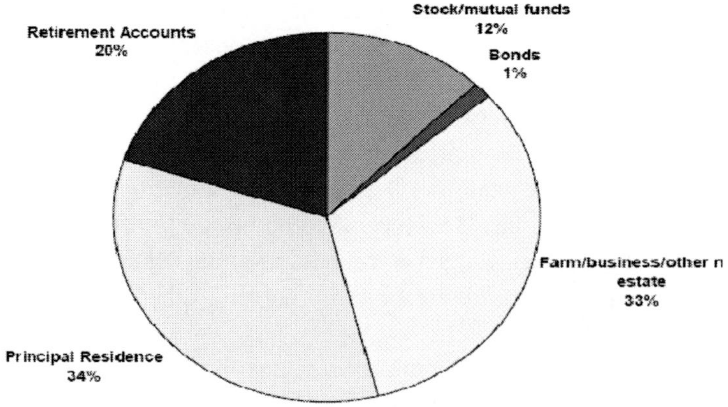

Source: CRS analysis of the 2007 SCF.

Figure 4. Assets Owned by Households, 2007.

Higher income households are more likely to own assets that can generate taxable capital gains than lower income households. Table 1 reports the proportion of households in each income category owning particular assets. For each type of asset, the proportion owning increases as income increases. For example, 7% of the poorest 20% of households own stocks or mutual funds compared to 72% of the richest 5% of households.

Table 1. Percentage Owning Assets by Income, 2007

Income category	Stocks/mutual funds	Bonds	Farm, business, other real estate	Principal residence	Retirement accounts
Quintile 1	6.9%	0.3%	10.0%	40.5%	11.2%
Quintile 2	11.5	0.2	13.5	57.1	34.6
Quintile 3	20.5	1.1	24.2	72.5	56.9
Quintile 4	30.4	1.2	31.0	82.6	73.6
Quintile 5	52.2	5.4	51.7	90.7	87.1
Top 10%	59.9	9.3	64.6	92.6	89.8
Top 5%	71.9	13.7	75.7	93.8	91.4

Source: CRS analysis of the 2007 SCF.

Most of the assets are owned by higher income households. Well over half of the assets that can generate taxable capital gains are owned by the richest 5% of households (see **Table 2**). Principal residences are more broadly distributed in the income distribution than other assets, but most of the gains from the sale of homes is excluded from federal taxation.

Table 2. Distribution of Assets by Income, 2007

Income category	Stocks/mutual funds	Bonds	Farm, business, other	Principal residence	Retirement Accounts
Quintile 1	1.0%	0.7%	3.1%	4.9%	0.4%
Quintile 2	1.5	0.2	3.0	9.1	2.4
Quintile 3	4.2	2.0	5.1	15.0	7.0
Quintile 4	10.2	3.8	9.5	22.0	20.4
Quintile 5	83.0	93.3	79.2	49.1	69.8
Top 10%	75.9	89.5	71.3	33.1	51.3
Top 5%	66.4	85.5	60.8	22.3	37.4

Source: CRS analysis of the 2007 SCF.

The distribution of capital accruals tends to follow the same pattern as the distribution of asset ownership. Table 3 reports the distribution of accrued capital gains for selected assets.[11] Capital gains accruals for stocks, mutual funds, and businesses are highly skewed toward the upper income levels. About 90% of capital gains accruals go to households in the richest income quintile and 70% go to the richest 5% of households. Capital gains accruals on principal residences, however, are less skewed—only 47% go to households in the richest income quintile.

Table 3. Accrued Capital Gains by Income, 2007

Income category	Stocks/mutual funds	Businesses	Other real estate	Principal residences
Quintile 1	0.7%	1.8%	3.3%	5.5%
Quintile 2	0.6	2.0	4.1	9.9
Quintile 3	1.5	2.8	8.2	16.0
Quintile 4	7.0	5.6	14.0	21.2
Quintile 5	90.2	87.8	70.4	47.4
Top 10%	85.4	80.6	60.0	31.6
Top 5%	75.7	69.2	49.4	20.9

Source: CRS analysis of the 2007 SCF.

Capital Gains Realizations and Taxes

The distribution of realized capital gains can be examined by one of two methods. First, the focus can be on how capital gains are distributed among all households. This allows for an examination of how income from capital gains is distributed throughout the entire income distribution.

Second, the focus can be narrowed to examine how realized capital gains are distributed among taxpayers—the group that reports income from capital gains. Many lower income individuals and families, such as those with income primarily from public assistance or Social Security, do not file tax returns and would be excluded from the analysis. Both methods are employed.

Income from realized capital gains, while always concentrated at the top of the income distribution, has become more concentrated over the past 25 years. Figure 5 displays the distribution of realized capital gains among all households (whether or not they filed tax returns) since 1979. In 1979, households in the bottom 95% of the income distribution received about 20% of total capital gains income (the dark grey and white bars). The richest 0.1% of households (about 81,000 households) received 36% of total capital gains income. By 2005, the bottom 95% received only 10% of total capital gains income while the richest 0.1% (about 114,000 households) received 50%.

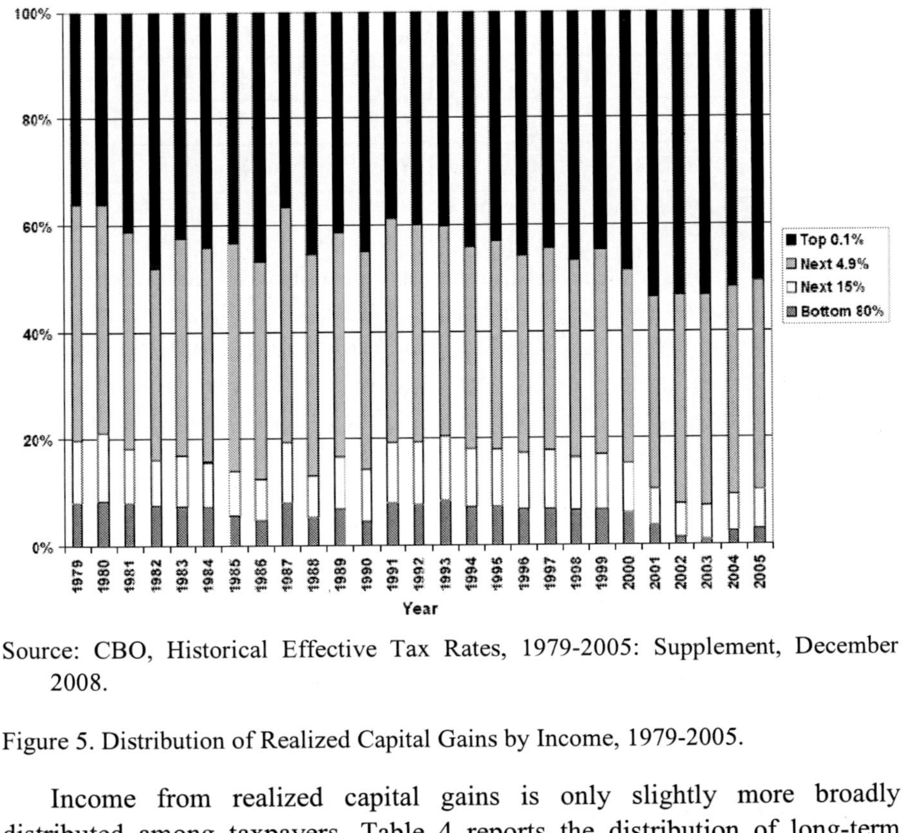

Source: CBO, Historical Effective Tax Rates, 1979-2005: Supplement, December 2008.

Figure 5. Distribution of Realized Capital Gains by Income, 1979-2005.

Income from realized capital gains is only slightly more broadly distributed among taxpayers. Table 4 reports the distribution of long-term capital gains and all capital gains in 2004. Longterm capital gains are taxed at preferential rates while short-term capital gains are not. About 18% of total long-term capital gains were received by taxpayers in the bottom 80% of the income distribution. Taxpayers in the top 20% received about 82% of total long-term capital gains and taxpayers in the richest 5% received 68% of total capital gains in 2004.

Table 4. Capital Gains Income and Capital Gains Taxes, 2004

Income category	Long-term capital gains	All capital gains	Taxes paid on capital gains
Quintile 1	2.7%	2.8%	1.4%
Quintile 2	3.3	3.5	2.1
Quintile 3	5.2	5.4	3.7
Quintile 4	6.9	7.0	6.1
Quintile 5	81.9	81.3	86.7
Top 10%	74.6	74.2	79.2
Top 5%	68.2	67.5	71.7

Source: 2004 IRS SOI PUF.

The final column of Table 4 reports the distribution of capital gains taxes (on both short-term and long-term capital gains). Overall, the distributional pattern is similar to the capital gains income distribution, but slightly more skewed toward the higher income levels. The primary reason is that lower income taxpayers faced a 5% long-term capital gains tax rate in 2004 while higher income taxpayers faced a 15% tax rate.

Economic Issues

Capital gains tax reductions are often proposed as a policy that will increase saving and investment, provide a short-term economic stimulus, and boost long-term economic growth. Each of these arguments is examined.

Saving and Investment

National saving is made up of saving by the government (public saving) and by households and firms (private saving). Public saving is equal to the government's deficit or surplus—it is negative for a deficit and positive for a surplus. Reducing capital gains tax rates will likely reduce public saving because it reduces tax revenues without affecting outlays; this increases a budget deficit or decreases a budget surplus.[12]

Households save by investing in their own business or investing in stocks, bonds, and other financial instruments. Changing capital gains tax rates changes the after-tax rate of return on investments (for example, reducing the tax rate increases the after-tax return). The change in the rate of return has two offsetting effects on saving.

Increasing the rate of return can increase households' willingness to save (the substitution effect). But at the same time, the increased return allows households to save less to maintain their desired or target wealth level (the income effect). Consequently, the effect of capital gains taxes on private saving is likely to be small.

The traditional economic theory of saving, the life-cycle model, assumes that individuals make rational, far-sighted decisions. The preponderance of empirical evidence, however, does not support the life-cycle model.[13] Behavioral theories of saving emphasize the role of inertia, the lack of self-control, and the limit of human intellectual capabilities. To cope with the complexities involved in making saving decisions, individuals often use simple rules of thumb and develop target levels of wealth.

Once their target level of wealth is obtained, many individuals suspend active saving.[14] Saving rates have fallen over the past 30 years while the capital gains tax rate has fallen from 28% in 1987 to 15% today (0% for taxpayers in the 10% and 15% tax brackets). This suggests that changing capital gains tax rates have had little effect on private saving.

Some have argued that preferential capital gains tax rates will boost high risk investments such as in venture capital. Most venture capital, however, is supplied by pension funds, college endowments, foundations, and insurance companies—sources not associated with the capital gains tax. In 2003, only about 10% of investors in venture capital funds were individuals and families.[15]

Additionally, for risk adverse investors, the capital gains tax could act as an insurance for risky investments by reducing losses as well as gains—it decreases the variability of returns.[16] The $3,000 loss limit may reduce the insurance value of the capital gains tax. But research has shown that almost three-quarters of taxpayers with capital losses were not subject to the loss limit because losses were less than $3,000 or gains offset the losses.[17]

Of those affected by the loss limit, two-thirds were able to deduct losses against gains or other income within two years. The capital gains tax, therefore, may have little effect on risk-taking and may even encourage it.

Capital gains tax rate reductions appear to decrease public saving and may have little or no effect on private saving. Consequently, capital gains tax reductions likely have a negative overall impact on national saving.

Economic Growth

Some have argued that reducing capital gains tax rates would increase short-run and long-run economic growth.[18] The long-run level of output depends on the amount of saving and investment. Saving and investment increase the amount of capital in the economy and hence, aggregate supply (i.e., the amount of goods and services available in the economy).

Many economists note that capital gains tax reductions appear to have little or even a negative effect on saving and investment (see above). Consequently, capital gains tax rate reductions are unlikely to have much effect on the long-term level of output or the path to the long-run level of output (i.e., economic growth).

Furthermore, it is argued that a temporary or permanent capital gains tax reduction is an effective economic stimulus measure. An effective short-term economic stimulus, however, will have to increase aggregate demand, which requires additional spending. A tax reduction on capital gains would mostly benefit very high income taxpayers who are likely to save most of any tax reduction.[19]

Economists note that a temporary capital gains tax reduction possibly could have a negative impact on short-term economic growth. A temporary tax cut could induce investors to sell stock (i.e., realize capital gains by reducing the lock-in effect), but provides no incentive to invest since investors know they will face higher tax rates in the future. To the extent that the resulting sell-off depresses stock prices, consumer confidence, already low during recessions, could be further undermined thus reducing consumer spending.

A permanent capital gains tax cut will likely have two offsetting effects on stock prices. There is the demand-side capitalization effect—investors would be willing to pay a higher price for assets on which they would pay lower capital gains taxes in the future (in essence shifting out the demand curve).

But there is also the supply-side lock-in effect in which investors would be willing to sell at a lower price because they have to pay lower capital gains taxes (in essence shifting out the supply curve). The ultimate effect on stock returns depends on the relative magnitude of these two effects, but it would likely be small in either direction.

Appendix. Data Sources

Two data sources are used in the analysis. The first is the 2007 Survey of Consumer Finances (SCF), which is prepared by the Federal Reserve Board. The SCF includes detailed information on household demographics, income, and wealth. In the analysis, households are ranked in the income distribution and assigned to income categories (quintiles) by their equivalence-adjusted household income, which is household income divided by the square root of family size. Each income quintile contains 20% of the households; in addition, the richest 10% (decile) and richest 5% (ventile) are included in the analysis. This adjustment controls for economies of scale within the household. Household income consists of income from all sources including public assistance, but excludes capital gains. All households are represented in the SCF sample regardless of whether or not they paid taxes.

Some analysts argue that capital gains income can temporarily make a low or moderate income household appear rich. To the extent that this is true, most capital gains income will appear to be received solely by the rich. Consequently, capital gains income is excluded from household income when assigning households to income categories. Most individuals and families, however, are in the same income category regardless of capital gains income—92% remain in the same quintile and 77% remain in the same ventile.

The second data source is the IRS's 2004 Statistics of Income Public Use File (SOI PUF). The SOI PUF contains information from the tax returns of a representative sample of taxpayers. Individuals and families that do not file a tax return are not included in this data source. These individuals and families are not required to file a tax return because of low income or receive primarily nontaxable income (e.g., public assistance). Taxpayers are assigned to income categories based on equivalence-adjusted total income; total income excludes capital gains income.

End Notes

[1] See Henry C. Simons, *Personal Income Taxation* (Chicago: University of Chicago Press, 1938).

[2] Capital assets are defined in Section 1221 of the Internal Revenue Code and explained in IRS publication 544. IRS publication 544 (p. 19) simply states that "[a]lmost everything you own and use for personal purposes or investment is a capital asset."

[3] See CRS Report RL31562, *An Analysis of the Tax Treatment of Capital Losses*, by Thomas L. Hungerford and Jane G. Gravelle.

[4] Martin Feldstein, Joel Slemrod, and Shlomo Yitzhaki, "The Effects of Taxation on the Selling of Corporate Stock and the Realizations of Capital Gains," *Quarterly Journal of Economics*, vol. 94, no. 4 (June 1980), p. 790.

[5] The authors note the problem of using cross-sectional data: "An individual whose tax rate varies substantially from year to year will tend to sell more when his rate is low. To the extent that low rates in 1973 are only temporarily low, our estimates will overstate the sensitivity of selling to the tax rate. We have no way of knowing how important this is" (p. 785).

[6] See Leonard E. Burman, *Labyrinth of Capital Gains Tax Policy: A Guide for the Perplexed* (Washington: Brookings Institution Press, 1999) and Jane G. Gravelle, *The Economic Effects of Taxing Capital Income* (Cambridge, MA: MIT Press, 1994) for discussions of this issue.

[7] Alan J. Auerbach, "Capital Gains Taxation and Tax Reform," *National Tax Journal*, vol. 42, no. 3 (1989), pp. 391-401. Auerbach concludes that "a permanent revenue increase [from a capital gains tax rate reduction] is unlikely enough to be discarded as a reason for reducing the capital gains tax rate" (p. 391).

[8] Jane G. Gravelle, "Limits to Capital Gains Feedback Effects," *Tax Notes*, vol. 51 (April 22, 1991), pp. 363-371.

[9] Gerald E. Auten and Charles T. Clotfelter, "Permanent versus Transitory Tax Effects and the Realization of Capital Gains," *Quarterly Journal of Economics*, vol. 97, no. 4 (November 1982), pp. 613-632.

[10] Leonard E. Burman and William C. Randolph, "Measuring Permanent Responses to Capital-Gains Tax Changes in Panel Data," *American Economic Review*, vol. 84, no. 4 (September 1994), pp. 794-809.

[11] The 2007 SCF doesn't allow capital gains accruals for other assets to be calculated.

[12] See Jane G. Gravelle, "Can A Capital Gains Tax Cut Pay for Itself," *Tax Notes*, vol. 48 (July 9, 1990), pp. 209-219.

[13] For a discussion and citations to the literature see CRS Report RL33482, *Saving Incentives: What May Work, What May Not*, by Thomas L. Hungerford.

[14] F. Thomas Juster, Joseph P. Lupton, James P. Smith, and Frank Stafford, "The Decline in Household Saving and the Wealth Effect," *Review of Economics and Statistics*, vol. 87, no. 4 (November 2005), pp. 20-27.

[15] National Venture Capital Association, *Venture Impact*, 4th Edition, 2007, available at http://www.nvca.org/pdf/ NVCA_VentureCapital07-2nd.pdf.

[16] See Burman, *Labyrinth of Capital Gains Tax Policy*.

[17] Alan J. Auerbach, Leonard E. Burman, and Jonathan M. Siegel, "Capital Gains Taxation and Tax Avoidance: New Evidence from Panel Data," in *Does Atlas Shrug?* ed. Joel B. Slemrod (Cambridge, MA: Harvard University Press, 2000), pp. 355-388.

[18] See, for example, Karen A. Campbell and Guinevere Nell, *Sustainable Economic Stimulus: Repeal Capital Gains and Dividend Taxes*, The Heritage Foundation, Web Memo no. 2263, February 3, 2009.

[19] See Jonathan McCarthy, "Imperfect Insurance and Differing Propensities to Consume Across Households," *Journal of Monetary Economics*, vol. 36, no. 2 (November 1995), pp. 301-327 for evidence that the wealthy have higher marginal propensities to save than low wealth households.

In: Capital Gains Taxation
Editors: M. Zimmerman, L. Curtis
ISBN: 978-1-62081-076-7

Chapter 3

CAPITAL GAINS TAX OPTIONS: BEHAVIORAL RESPONSES AND REVENUES*

Jane G. Gravelle

SUMMARY

Among the expiring Bush tax cut provisions is a lower 15% rate for long-term capital gains and dividends, with a 0% rate for taxpayers with ordinary tax rates of 15% or less. With no change, capital gains tax rates will revert to a top rate of 20% (10% for those with a 0% rate). Dividends will be taxed at ordinary rates. For FY2010 (for example), Treasury has projected revenue gains from these provisions to be $16 billion for capital gains and $30 billion for dividends.

President Obama has proposed to retain the 15% and 0% rates for lower- and middle-income taxpayers, but to tax both dividends and capital gains at 20% for married couples with income of $250,000 or more and single taxpayers with income of $200,000 or more. Because the increase in dividend tax rates was limited, about 80% of the projected $15 billion gain from this revision (for FY2019) is estimated to be from capital gains tax increases.

Compared with most other tax provisions, the potential revenue gain scored for an increase in capital gains taxes is strongly affected by behavioral

* This is an edited, reformatted and augmented version of a Congressional Research Service publication, CRS Report for Congress R41364, dated August 10, 2010.

responses assumed by the Joint Committee on Taxation (JCT) and the Treasury Department. The analysis in this study suggests that the Administration's projections and those of the JCT, absent a change in their realizations response, may likely understate revenue gains from allowing lower capital gains tax rates to expire.

Realizations responses were first added to revenue projections by the revenue estimating agencies (Joint Committee on Taxation and the Treasury) at the end of the 1 980s, in the midst of a contentious debate. The larger the absolute value of the elasticity (the percentage change in realizations divided by the percentage change in taxes) the smaller the revenue gain, and with elasticities larger than one in absolute value, a loss would occur. Estimated elasticities in the literature prior to 1990 ranged from 0.3 to almost 3.8, leaving limited guidance for revenue estimating agencies. JCT used an elasticity of 0.76, whereas Treasury used an elasticity of one.

Concerns were raised at that time that there were serious problems with this evidence. Perhaps the most significant concern was that the larger results from studies of individuals reflected a timing or transitory response (high income taxpayers with variable income chose to realize gains during times that tax rates were temporarily low). This transitory response is not appropriate for assessing a permanent change.

Evidence and studies since that time suggest that the permanent elasticity is considerably lower than what appeared to be the case in 1990. The surge in realizations in 1986 as a capital gains tax rate increase was preannounced provided compelling evidence of the importance of a transitory response. A study of the limits of realizations (which cannot exceed accruals in the long run) suggested the elasticity could be no more than 0.5. And a number of new econometric studies, using new techniques to isolate the permanent response, suggested elasticities of around 0.5 or less. The JCT appears to maintain their original assumption, while the Treasury response has been reduced to be similar to JCT's.

Although projected revenues for FY2019 would be smaller than that estimated in January 2010 by the Administration, due to the Medicare tax, the revenue gain from allowing the capital gains tax to rise could be up to twice as much as that projected by the JCT for FY2019 if the smaller responses estimated in more recent studies were applied. It is reasonable to expect revenue gains of $28 billion, rather than the $13 billion likely to be projected by JCT if they maintain their current realizations response assumptions, and the gain is unlikely to be less than $18 billion.

At the end of 2010, the Bush tax cuts, enacted in 2001 and 2003, will expire. Among the expiring tax provisions is a lower 15% rate for long term capital gains and dividends, with a 0% tax rate on capital gains and dividends for taxpayers subject to ordinary rates of 15% or less. With no change, capital gains tax rates will revert to pre-2003 rates of 20% and 10% (18% and 8% for assets held for five years or more), and dividends will be taxed at ordinary rates. The highest ordinary tax rate is currently 35% but, absent change, will rise to 39.6%.

President Obama proposed in both his budget outlines (FY2010 and FY2011) to retain the 15% and 0% rates for lower- and middle-income taxpayers, but to tax both dividends and capital gains at 20% for married couples with income of $250,000 or more and single taxpayers with income of $200,000 or more.

Compared with most other tax provisions, the potential revenue gain scored for an increase in capital gains taxes is strongly affected by behavioral responses assumed by the Joint Committee on Taxation (JCT) and the Treasury Department. As an illustration, the Administration estimated in February 2010 that revenue raised by allowing expiration of the Bush tax cuts would be $16 billion in FY2019.[1] Yet, based on Congressional Budget Office (CBO) projections in January 2010, the current effective capital gains tax was 13.3% in 2008 and would rise to 17.9% in 2019; applying the differential in these rates to the realizations in 2019 would produce a revenue difference of $40 billion.[2] Although some of this differential could arise from different forecasts, the main reason for the reduction in projected revenues by is due to assumptions about behavioral responses.

Realizations responses were first added to revenue projections by the revenue estimating agencies (JCT and Treasury) at the end of the 1980s, in the midst of a contentious debate. This report explains how these responses affect revenues, discusses the debate that occurred in the late 1980s, reviews research since that time, and analyzes the implications for revenue effects.[3] The analysis in this report suggests that the Administration's projections and those of the JCT, absent a change in their realizations response, may likely understate revenue gains from allowing lower capital gains tax rates to expire.

REALIZATIONS RESPONSES AND REVENUE

Because taxpayers can choose to realize capital gains, economists and policy makers have been concerned about a reduction in the potential revenue from capital gains taxes because those taxes reduce realizations. It is possible for a tax increase to lose revenue if the response is large enough.

If realizations are postponed until death, the gains escape tax entirely.[4] Thus, there is an incentive to delay and perhaps ultimately avoid the tax by not selling assets.

Capital gains realizations responses are typically expressed in the form of an elasticity, which is the percentage change in realizations divided by the percentage change in taxes. These elasticities are expected to be negative but are often reported without the minus sign (and will be in this report). If realizations increase by 5% when the tax rate falls by 10%, the elasticity is 0.5; if realizations increase by 10% when the tax rate falls by 10%, the elasticity is one; if realizations rise by 20% while the tax rate falls by 10%, the elasticity is two.

The higher the value of the elasticity, the smaller the revenue gain or loss from a capital gains tax increase or decrease. If the elasticity is less than one, a tax increase gains revenue; if the elasticity is greater than one, the tax increase loses revenue. For a small increase in tax rates, the ratio of revenue gain projected to the gain realized with no behavioral response (static gain) is one minus the elasticity. Thus, if the elasticity is 0.25, 75% of the static revenue gain will be realized (that is (1-0.25) times the static gain). If the elasticity is 1.25, the tax increase will *lose* 25% of the static gain (i.e., (1-1.25) equals minus 0.25).[5]

Three types of elasticities are relevant to capital gains realizations and revenues and are discussed in the economics literature. The first is the permanent elasticity, which is most relevant for permanent tax law changes: it measures the longer run (after a year or two) realizations response to a permanent change in tax rate. The second is the short-run elasticity, which measures the short term response to a permanent change. The third is the transitory elasticity which measures the response to a temporary tax increase or decrease. This transitory effect might occur because the incomes of wealthy individuals (and the associated taxes due) may vary from year to year, and they time realizations in years when their tax rates are low. It may also occur in the aggregate when a tax change is pre-announced. For example, if taxpayers learn that the tax is increasing next year, they may shift realizations into the current year to take advantage of this year's lower tax rate.

Although this discussion will focus on the magnitude and effects of permanent elasticities, these short-term and transitory effects constitute both a challenge in estimation and affect shorter-term responses to changes. Thus a brief discussion is in order.

The short-term realizations elasticity has most often been discussed (as it was in the late 1980s) in the context of a capital gains tax cut. The idea behind such as response is that taxpayers have a large stock of accrued gains that they would have already realized if the tax rate were lower and thus there will be a larger increase in realizations in the first year or two.

There are two caveats about applying such an effect. The first is that the short-term response may be muted if there has been a recent increase in realizations. For example, unbeknownst to revenue estimators in the late 1980s (because the data were not available), there had been a surge in realizations in 1986 because of the pre-announced increase in capital gains taxes for 1987 and later years as part of the Tax Reform Act of 1986. With so many of these accrued gains exhausted, it was unlikely that there would have been a very large short run response had a tax cut been enacted in 1990.

Second, and more important for the current issue, there is no reason to expect that short-run responses apply to a tax increase that is not pre-announced, because, although a cut in taxes may unleash significant short-term realizations from the existing stock of gains, an increase should not cause a similar contraction. The stock of gains that has not been realized because of taxes will simply remain unrealized, with no effect on realizations.[6]

The transitory response is sometimes used interchangeably with the short-term response, but transitory responses can be thought of as occurring because of a temporary lower or higher rate. As noted above, a large aggregate transitory response occurred in 1986 because of the passage of legislation that raised future tax rates significantly. However, because the higher-income taxpayers who realize most capital gains can have significant fluctuations in income and taxes, transitory responses occur among individuals even in years when the law does not change. This possibility of a transitory response was more pronounced in the period (prior to 1987) when capital gains were subject to graduated rates (because the tax benefit was an exclusion rather than a fixed rate).

Statistical estimates of realizations responses can be based on a variety of functional forms, but one of the most common functions causes the elasticity (percentage change in gains divided by a percentage change in tax rates) to rise proportionally with the tax rate. Therefore elasticities should be reported with reference to the assumed tax rate. For much of the discussion in the 1990 debate, the relevant tax rate was the one associated with the tax change under consideration, the 22% rate midway between the current and new rate. Many elasticities discussed at that time reflect that rate. Capital gains realizations elasticities are expected to be negative but the elasticities in this report will be stated and referred to in absolute value (without the minus sign).

This formulation also leads to a revenue maximizing tax rate, which is the tax rate at which the most capital gains tax revenue will be realized. The underlying equations are presented in **Appendix A**.

For considering the effects of allowing the current Bush tax cut to expire, the tax rate at which elasticities are valued would be slightly lower than was the case in 1990 and thus larger revenue gains are more likely. According to CBO projections, the effective tax rate on capital gains under the current regime is 13.3% and the tax rate if the cuts expire is 17.9%.[7] The recent health legislation added a 3.8% Medicare tax on capital income (including capital gains) for taxpayers with incomes above $250,000 for couples and $200,000 for singles. Assuming that about 81% of capital gains is affected, the tax rates would rise by 3.1 percentage points, leading to rates of 16.4% and 21.0%. The midpoint of these amounts is 18.7%.[8] Thus, elasticities at this rate would be 85% of those commonly reported in 1990.

Note that these issues surrounding capital gains taxes and realizations are not applicable to taxes on dividends, and fewer dividends (about 50%) are subject to the additional 3.8% tax. Dividends would return, absent change, to ordinary rates and the revenue gain from that change is $30 billion; hence, the gain from expiration of tax cuts on both dividends and capital gains is projected by the Administration at $46 billion. The Administration's proposal (to raise rates only for those with incomes over $200,000 (single) and $250,000 (married)) would raise only a third of the total, $15 billion, partly because of the limited coverage of taxpayers and partly because the proposal retains part of the benefit for dividends by taxing them at 20% rather than at ordinary rates. Only about $3 billion of the potential $30 billion revenue from raising taxes on dividends is estimated to be collected, with the remainder (8 0%) of the $15 billion of revenue in the Administration's proposal from capital gains.[9] Thus the capital gains portion is much more important in the Adminstration's proposal and is estimated to account for 80% of the total revenue from allowing capital gains tax cuts to expire.

THE 1990 DEBATE

In 1990, the George H. W. Bush Administration proposed to reduce the capital gains tax rate that had been adopted in 1986. That legislation increased the top rate on capital gains from 20% to 28% by taxing capital gains as ordinary income. During the late 1980s, the revenue estimating agencies (the Joint Committee on Taxation and the Treasury Department's Office of Tax Analysis) had begun to investigate and add behavioral responses in the form of realizations elasticities. The Congressional Budget Office also began to include tax variables in their regressions used to forecast baseline capital gains revenues.

Because of the strict budget constraints applying at that time, the issue of revenue cost was a crucial one in 1990.[10] The Administration chose an elasticity (at a 22% rate) of 0.98. The JTC used an elasticity of 0.76.[11]

Two types of data were used to estimate the realizations response. The first was aggregate time series, which related total realizations in different years to the tax rate in that year.

The second was micro-data studies which examined individual taxpayers' realizations in comparison to their tax rates. These studies included cross-section studies (which compare taxpayers in a single year), pooled cross-section time-series (which compare taxpayers and include many years but do not follow individual taxpayers over time) and panel studies (which compare taxpayers over time, tracking each taxpayer).

As shown in **Table B-1** in **Appendix B**, estimates of the realizations response varied dramatically, from 0.3 to almost 4. To make the revenue implications clear, an elasticity of 0.3 would imply, for a small increase in the tax rate, that the revenue gained would be 70% of the revenue projected if there were no realizations response.

An elasticity of 4 implies a *loss* of three times the projected revenue gained if there were no behavioral response. Estimates based on aggregate time series were generally lower, ranging from 0.3 to 0.9 (70% to 10% of revenue gained). Estimates based on individual taxpayer data ranged from 0.55 to 3.8.

The range of estimated responses and their implications for revenue implied serious problems with the estimation methods. The range was particularly broad for estimates based on individual data.

The JCT took the position that the time series results were more reliable and they estimated their own elasticity using this methodology. The Treasury never actually provided a specific methodology for their number, but rather reported it as a conservative choice given the realizations estimates.

Researchers trying to estimate the realizations response faced many problems, which are discussed in more detail in **Appendix B**. In general, individual data are preferred for estimation, because aggregation can produce a bias and loses information. In addition, it is very difficult to control for other factors that change over time.

More important, for using individual data, was the problem of distinguishing between permanent and transitory responses. Because income, especially of high-income individuals who realize most gains, can fluctuate over time, tax rates also vary over time. Individuals would be expected to time realizations to coincide with periods of low rates.

Individuals might also need to cash in assets when income (and therefore taxes) is unusually low. This concern basically precluded relying on simple cross-section results for permanent responses.

Thus, no revenue estimating entity relied on the larger elasticities (close to 4) produced by some of these micro-data studies.

Arguments were made at the time that panel data, which followed individuals over a several years, could be used to separate these elasticities, since in these data individual tax rates could be examined over several years. These studies used the average of the current, previous, and future tax rate as a permanent rate.

These studies reported smaller elasticities, but ones that still were well above one in some cases.

Because of an incorrectly reported elasticity, the three panel studies available at that time appeared to produce a much narrower range of results. These panel results probably influenced the Treasury to choose a larger elasticity than those suggested by the aggregate time series data.

However, as noted in the following section, the last panel study also had a very large elasticity.[12] Thus, although attempts were made to address the problem of transitory effects with panel studies, this procedure may not correct for the transitory effect, perhaps because periods of lower income or higher income can continue for several years.

Although panel studies offered some possibility of controlling for transitory effects, the panels available were for only a few years. If the higher-income individuals who realize most gains experienced prolonged spells of higher or lower than normal income, panel studies might reduce the transitory element, but estimates could still reflect some transitory response elements. Thus panel estimates could still be too large, whereas the biases in time-series estimates remained uncertain. Neither approach was without flaws.

Ultimately the proposed tax cuts were not enacted at that time (although they were eventually reduced in 1997 and again in 2003).

DEVELOPMENTS SINCE 1990

The range of realizations elasticities, even if confined to time series estimates, is very broad for revenue estimating purposes or otherwise evaluating capital gains taxes. Researchers turned their attention to methods to produce more precise and reliable estimates.

One important event that influenced thinking about these elasticities was the sharp spike in realizations that occurred in 1986. Between 1985 and 1986, realizations rose from $170.6 billion to $324.4 billion, falling to $144.2 billion in 1987.[13] A study of this phenomenon using taxpayer data showed that these gains occurred in December, and were seven times the gains in December of the previous year. [14] This increase, which took place when a tax increase was passed for the following years, was evidence of the magnitude of transitory realizations responses and contributed further to concerns about the reflection of transitory responses in the econometric studies.

Eight additional econometric studies of the realizations response have been identified beginning in 1990, and six of those studies are reported in **Table 1**.[15] The table also includes estimates of current practices by CBO, JCT, and Treasury. [16] The CBO realizations estimate is continually estimated as new data emerge, but its object, CBO cautions, is not for the purpose of estimating revenues. Rather, the tax rate is included as part of an overall statistical study which includes many variables used to project capital gains realizations for the baseline. [17]

The second column of **Table 1** reports the coefficient which, multiplied by the tax rate, will produce the elasticity. The studies are arrayed by elasticity, from smallest to largest.

Table 1 also includes the results of a study by Gravelle, which was not an econometric study.[18] Some analysts had observed that large estimated elasticities from cross-section and panel studies implied large realizations that were far outside the scope of historical experience.[19] Gravelle's study noted that there was a limit to the realizations response, in that, for a permanent elasticity, realizations could not exceed accruals (the change in the market value of assets). If every asset were sold every year, realizations would equal accruals, but they could be no larger. The study provided data on the ratio of realizations to accruals, along with tax rates, over a long period of time, and used the average values to estimate the upper limit of the realizations elasticity. The study found that limit to be 0.5, below the estimates of all of the existing cross-section and panel studies, and below most of the time series studies. Moreover, the 0.5 limit is an upper limit and implies that in the absence of taxes and transactions costs individuals would sell every asset every year. Since some assets are unlikely to be sold even in those circumstances because investors are satisfied with their investments, the elasticity is likely to be considerably lower. **Table 1**, therefore, reports both the upper limit and the midpoint of this study.

Table 1. Realizations Elasticities, Post-1980s Studies

Sources of Data	Coefficient	Realizations Elasticity at 22%	Realizations Elasticity at 18.7%
No Change in Behavior	0.0	0.00	0.00
Burman and Randolph Panel Study (1994)	1.0	0.22	0.19
Auerbach and Siegel Panel Study (2000)	1.126	0.25	0.21
Gravelle Limit Study Midpoint (1991)	1.136	0.25	0.21
CBO Time Series (Current)	1.76	0.39	0.33
Gravelle Limit Study Upper Limit (1991)	2.27	0.5	0.42
Eichner and Sinai Time Series (2000)	2.28	0.5	0.43
Bogart and Gentry Cross-State (2000)	2.5	0.55	0.47
JCT	3.1	0.68	0.58
Treasury	3.25	0.72	0.61
Gillingham and Greenlees Time Series (1992)	3.4	0.75	0.64
Auten and Joulfain Panel Study (2004)	3.6	0.79	0.67

Source: See **Appendix B** for summaries of studies and **Appendix C** for citations.

Notes: The coefficient is the fixed estimate from a semi-log function that, multiplied by the tax rate, yields the elasticity. That is, if the regression is of the form: log gain = a + bt + other regressors, and t is the tax rate, the coefficient is b. It is expected to be negative but is reported as an absolute value.

That same study also corrected the elasticity for the most recent panel study of the 1 980s, indicating an elasticity of 3.2, similar to the cross-section results.[20] This correction reinforced the observation that the panel studies could not necessarily address the transitory issues that plagued cross-section studies.

Three of the six studies are panel studies, two are times series, and one is a cross-state aggregate study. The Burman and Randolph study was perhaps the most innovative econometric study because it used variation in state tax rates to estimate the permanent elasticity. That study found a very small elasticity that was statistically insignificant and a very large (in excess of 6) transitory elasticity. Because state tax rates are exogenous and presumed permanent, their evidence suggested a very small response. Auerbach and Siegel replicated their approach with different years and found similar results. The findings in these studies were consistent with the Gravelle estimate of limits in that they fell below the upper limit of elasticities. Most subsequent studies have incorporated state tax rates.

The Auten and Joulfaian panel study, by contrast, had the highest elasticity of any of the studies. There were two aspects that were likely to lower their elasticities compared with earlier panel studies: they added state tax rates and they had a much longer panel so that time series effects probably became more important. Their study, however, continued the approach used by earlier panel studies that used adjacent years to capture permanent tax rates. This period may be too short and for that reason, their estimates probably continue to reflect transitory, timing responses. These timing responses are not appropriate for measuring a permanent response.

Two of the studies (along with CBO's estimate) used aggregate times series data. The Gillingham and Greenlees study was the earliest and added a few years of data to some earlier studies, whereas the other time series studies (Eichner and Sinai) added many more years. Both studies control for 1986, which was an unusual year. It appears that more years added to time series data lead to lower elasticities; however, all of the time series results fall within the range of the eight time series studies from the 1980s. One time series study falls below the upper limit estimated by Gravelle, one is about at the upper limit, and one is considerably larger.

The third study, by Bogart and Gentry, used aggregate data over time grouped by state. Because they include time controls, they also relied on cross-state variation to identify a permanent response. Their results were slightly above the Gravelle study's upper limit.

The elasticities in **Table 1** are closer together and lower than those in the studies of the 1980s. JCT's current coefficient appears to be similar to the estimate used during the 1990 debate (although the elasticity was slightly higher in 1990, that appears to be due to the exclusion of small portfolio effects;[21] without those, it would probably be around 0.76). The Treasury estimate has been reduced and is now of the same rough magnitude as the JCT assumption.

Given the evidence from panel studies that use state variation to identify permanent effects and studies of the reasonableness of elasticities given realizations responses, both JCT and Treasury estimates appear high, so that they likely understate the revenue to be gained from allowing the Bush tax cuts to expire.

Table 2 uses the elasticities from **Table 1** and the CBO projections to compare these revenue estimates for 2019, based on these results. The CBO projection was first modified to adjust for CBO's realizations elasticity, so as to begin with a (higher) static projection of realizations. That led to a revenue gain, absent a realizations response of $43 billion (slightly larger than the revenue from applying the tax change to the CBO baseline number). For the remaining revenue estimates, two changes were made in each case. First, the starting baseline was adjusted for the different elasticities to reflect the Medicare tax. Then the formula for revenues was applied to each baseline. The ratios in the last column do not adjust for initial baseline differences but just reflect the relative effects across estimates of allowing the tax cuts to expire, starting from a common baseline.

Note that the Treasury estimate is somewhat smaller, $14 billion, than that projected in January 2010 by the Administration. This difference is largely due to the smaller baseline and increase in elasticity due to the Medicare tax.

Table 2. Revenue Gain from Allowing Capital Gains Tax Rates to Expire, Estimates for FY2019 Based on Alternative Realizations Responses

Sources of Data	Revenue Gain 2019 ($billions)	Ratio of Revenue Gain to Static Gain
No Response	43.1	1.00
Burman and Randolph Panel Study (1994)	33.1	0.79
Auerbach and Siegel Panel Study (2000)	31.8	0.77
Gravelle Limit Study Midpoint (1991)	31.7	0.77
CBO Time Series (Current)	26.0	0.64
Gravelle Limit Study Upper Limit (1991)	21.8	0.55
Eichner and Sinai Time Series (2000)	21.6	0.55
Bogart and Gentry Cross-State (2000)	19.8	0.50
JCT	15.1	0.39
Treasury	13.9	0.37
Gillingham and Greenlees Time Series (1992)	12.8	0.34
Auten and Joulfaian Panel Study (2004)	11.4	0.30

Source: Estimates in Table 1 and Applications of Formulas in Appendix A.

Notes: The ratio of revenue gain reflects only the tax change assuming a common initial baseline. Projected revenue gain also adjusts the starting baseline for each case to reflect the Medicare tax.

As shown in **Table 2**, the revenue gain as a percentage of static gain ranges from a reduction of 20% to a reduction of 70%. The revenue gain for the expiration of the Bush capital gains tax cuts ranges, from the lowest to the highest elasticity, from $33.1 billion per year to $11.4 billion, a range of $21.7 billion.

Which results are most reliable? The Auten and Joulfaian panel study, judging by problems with short panels in the 1980s, probably retains some transitory elasticity effects because it applied the same methodology. Although it also reflects time series elements, the estimate is probably an overstatement of the permanent elasticity. It also substantially exceeds the upper limit estimated by Gravelle.

Turning to time series, the Eichner and Sinai results include many more years than Gillingham and Greenlees, suggesting that this time series result should be preferred. CBO includes even more years. Given the findings of the remaining studies and of Gravelle's limit calculations, the elasticity is likely below 0.5.

These findings suggest that revenue estimating assumptions retained from the 1990 debate may understate the revenue gain. In all cases, evidence from both post-1980s econometric studies and the limits study indicates that there will be revenue gains from allowing the lower tax rates on capital gains to expire. Revenue gained assuming the elasticities found by Burman and Randolph or Auerbach and Siegel, which may incorporate the best method of isolating the permanent elasticity and is consistent with the limit estimates of Gravelle, is twice the amount likely to be projected by the JCT. Using the Gravelle upper limit, revenues would be 45% larger. Thus, the Administration's projections and those of the JCT, absent a change in their realizations response, may likely understate revenue gains from allowing lower capital gains tax rates to expire.

APPENDIX A. MODELING REALIZATIONS AND REVENUES

The elasticity of realizations with respect to taxes can be estimated with a variety of functional forms, but one of the most common, and the one on which the estimates in Table 2 are based is a semi-log function of the form (excluding the constant and other regressors, such as stock market values and GDP):

$$\log G = bt \tag{1}$$

where G is gains, t is the tax rate, and b is the tax rate coefficient to be estimated. If equation (1) is differentiated, and b is restated in absolute value, the result is:

$$dG/G = -b\ dt \qquad (2)$$

Multiplying the right hand side top and bottom by t results in an elasticity (dG/G divided by dt/t) of bt. Since the relationship is normally negative, but it is convenient to restate b in absolute value, a minus sign is added to b.

If equation (1) is restated in its originally, non-logged form (again ignoring other explanatory variables and stating b in absolute value), it is:

$$G = A\ e\text{-}bt \qquad (3)$$

Since revenues are tG,, the revenue equation is written:

$$R = tAe^{-bt} \qquad (4)$$

Note that if equation (4) is logged and differentiated, the result is dR/r = dt/t (1-bt). Thus, if the absolute value of the elasticity bt, is 1, there is no revenue gain.

To estimate revenues, denoting new values with an *, divide new revenues by old to achieve:

$$R^* = R^*\ (t^*/t)e^{-b(t^*-t)} \qquad (5)$$

The revenue maximizing tax rate is where dR/R=0, or where (1-bt) equals zero. This rate is equal to 1/b. Thus, if the coefficient of b is two, the revenue maximizing tax rate is 50% and if b equals 5 the revenue maximizing tax rate is 20%.

APPENDIX B. ECONOMETRIC STUDIES

Elasticities in Studies of the 1980s

Table B-1 reports the elasticities found in a series of estimates of the realizations elasticity in the 1 980s, the information available to influence a choice of realizations response at the time of the 1990 debate. These studies are discussed in general terms earlier, and in more specific terms in the following subsection. Where possible elasticities are reported at a 22% tax rate. The studies are divided into categories based on the fundamental approach used. Citations to all studies in this report are in **Appendix C**.

Table B-1. Elasticities from Studies of the 1980s

Study	Elasticity
Aggregate Time Series	
Auten (1982)	0.80
Treasury (1985)	0.84
CBO (1986)	0.27
Darby, Gillingham, and Greenless (1988)	0.58
CBO (1988)	0.76
CBO Alternative (1988)	0.45
Auerbach (1989)	0.54
Jones (1989)	0.89
Micro-Data: Panel	
Auten and Clotfelter (1982)	0.55
Treasury (1985)	1.29
Auten, Burman, and Randolph (1989)	3.20
Micro-Data: Cross-Section	
Feldstein, Slemrod, and Yitzhaki (1980)	3.75
Minarik (1981)	0.62
Gillingham, Greenless, and Zeischang (1989)	3.80
Micro-Data: Pooled Cross-Section Time-Series	
Lindsey (1987)	1.18
Treasury Elasticity, 1989	0.98
Joint Committee on Taxation Elasticity, 1989	0.76

Source: Table Reproduced from Table 2 in Jane Gravelle "Can A Capital Gains Tax Cut Pay for Itself?" *Tax Notes* 48, July 9, 1990, pp. 209-219. The elasticity for the Auten, Burman, Randolph panel study was revised from 1.65 to 3.2 reflecting the discussion in Jane Gravelle, "Limits to Capital Gains Feedback Effects," *Tax Notes* 51, April 22, 1991, pp. 363-371

General Issues

Statistical (or econometric) studies relating capital gains realizations to tax rates face many challenges and some of the debate over the evidence reflects the concerns about these challenges. The debate also concerned which type of data should be used: aggregate time series (which examines total economy-wide realizations over time compared with the economy-wide tax rates) versus individual taxpayer data (which related individual realizations to individual tax rates). As can be seen in **Table B-1**, aggregate time series results were generally smaller and more consistent, falling within a range of 0.3 to 0.9. Estimates based on micro data (individual observations) varied from 0.55 to almost 4.[22] The estimate for the pooled time-series, cross- section regression probably reflects a mix of times series and cross-section results.

Other things equal, it is more desirable to use individual data, because aggregate data cause a loss of information (i.e., individual variability is lost when individual responses are aggregated) and can bias the results. In addition, it is difficult to control for all of the changes over time that can affect realizations. Two of these, changes in transactions costs and a disconnect between changes in asset prices and changes in accruals, could cause estimates to be overstated.[23] Nor is it clear that the times series estimates are capturing only permanent effects. Other effects, however, could work in the opposite direction.

Yet the problems associated with studies based on individual data sets were so severe that many researchers believed that aggregate time series results were more reliable.

As an initial problem and point of contention, the effective capital gains tax rate, which would be used as a predetermined (exogenous) variable to explain realizations in a regression, is actually an endogenous variable which is influenced by the amount of realizations itself. Different techniques could, in theory, be used to address this very serious econometric problem, including using the first dollar tax rate (the tax that would appear on the first dollar of capital gains), using maximum statutory rates, using a rate based on predicted gains (where predicted gains are based on other attributes) or using instrumental variables methods.[24] In general, these problems of endogeneity of the explanatory variable are much more severe in the case of individual cross-section data, where much of the variation is due to individual circumstances, and less important in aggregate time series data where the major source of variation is changes in the law.

As noted earlier, another important issue, for using individual data, was the problem of distinguishing between permanent and transitory responses. Because income, especially of high- income individuals who realize most gains, can fluctuate over time, tax rates also vary over time. Individuals would be expected to time realizations to coincide with periods of low rates.

Individuals might also need to cash in assets when income (and therefore taxes) is unusually low. Although attempts were made to address this problem with panel studies by averaging the previous year, current year, and next year tax rates to create a permanent rate, this procedure may not correct for the transitory effect, perhaps because periods of lower income can continue for several years.

Studies Since the 1980s

The following discussion reviews the realizations studies published since the 1980s. In some cases, studies used many specifications, and this section explains why specific results were reported in **Table 1**, and why results from two studies were not included. References to these studies are in **Appendix C**. They are discussed in order of publication.

Slemrod and Shobe (1990)

This study uses a six-year small panel to replicate the Feldstein, Slemrod, and Yitzhaki and the Auten and Clotfelter studies. The authors found varying, but quite large, elasticities (in excess of one, and in excess of five in some cases). Their study appears to confirm potential problems with these studies, and also suggests short panels have significant problems as well (as the elasticity for their full sample was 5.84). These large elasticities are similar to those from cross-section and some panel studies in the 1980s, although some were not statistically significant and results varied significantly over time periods.

Slemrod and Shobe also estimated a regression that related the difference between current year realizations and average realizations to the difference between current year and average tax rates. They also obtain large, but statistically insignificant results. They acknowledge that their results may capture transitory effects. Because this study continues a methodology that has largely been rejected, the results are excluded from **Table 1**.

Gillingham and Greenlees (1992)

This study extends a previous times series analysis covering 1954-1985 for a short period (through 1989) and makes some changes in approaches used by CBO to replicate the results. The CBO study referenced used tax rates based on predicted gains in a standard regression. The authors consider three changes. The first is to use an instrumental variables technique that uses taxes on predicted gains as an instrument (that is, first regress actual effective tax rates on predicted tax rates and use the fitted values in the regression on realizations). This provision increased the coefficient from 2.9 to 4.2 and increased the elasticity at a 22% tax rate, from 0.64 to 0.92. Second, they suggested use of the maximum tax rate as an instrument rather than the predicted tax rate, which increased the coefficient to 5.8 and the elasticity to 1.28. They also argued that the data should be differenced (a change in realizations related to a change in rates); differencing produced higher elasticities (1.39 for the instrument with predicted gains and 1.429 for the instrument with the maximum rate) but these elasticities were not statistically significant at conventional levels. Differencing may also capture short-term or transitory effects. Finally they extended the time period through 1989, with and without excluding 1986. Excluding 1986, they found an estimate of 3.4 rather than 4.2 using the predicted gains instrument and 3.5 when the data were differenced (corresponding to elasticities of 0.75 and 0.77 at a 22% rate). For the maximum rate, the values were 5.4 and 5.3 (with and without differencing) corresponding to elasticities of 1.18 and 1.16. Confining the elasticities under consideration to those in the extended sample but excluding 1986, the crucial issue is whether to use the predicted gains rate or the maximum rate as an instrument. It is difficult to know what conclusion to draw from this study, since the principal conclusion of the authors is that micro-data approaches are superior.

There are problems with using the maximum rate as an instrument for this time-series regression, because the law itself changed substantially over the time period in a way that altered the relationship between the maximum rate and the average rate. Over this time period, there were episodes where the maximum rate affected a large fraction of taxpayers and other periods where it affected only a small fraction of taxpayers. Given these reservations about using the maximum rate, the coefficient of 3.4 is reported in **Table 1**.

Burman and Randolph (1994)

The Burman and Randolph study is perhaps the most innovative study done since the 1980s. It separated permanent and transitory effects in a short panel (1979-1983) using variations in state tax rates to identify permanent effects. For the transitory rate, the authors included in their instruments the first dollar current tax rate, which introduced a transitory element. Thus taxpayers with unusually low current income, excluding capital gains (and low current first dollar rates) would have transitory rates below their permanent rates, whereas those with high income would have higher rates. The permanent rates would vary across taxpayers in different states due to state tax rates. The authors estimated at elasticity of 0.18 at an 18% tax rate, which implies a coefficient of one, and an elasticity of 0.22 at a 22% tax rate. This estimated effect was not statistically significant, probably because there was not very much variation in tax rates.[25] They estimated a transitory elasticity of 6.45. Several subsequent studies use across state variations or incorporate state tax rates into the analysis.

Bogart and Gentry (1995)

This study also relied on differentials across states to identify permanent responses, but used aggregate state level gains from 1979 to 1990. The study also uses year dummies to control for fixed-year effects, so that the basic identification is due largely to the differential in tax rates across states. The authors report an elasticity of 0.65, which at their reported tax rate reflects a coefficient of 2.5. For a 22% rate, this coefficient leads to an elasticity of 0.55. The techniques used in the study should identify a permanent elasticity.

Auerbach and Siegel (2000)

Auerbach and Siegel used panel data from 1985 to 1994 to replicate the Burman and Randolph results for a different time period. They report an elasticity of 0.33 at the mean of the tax rate. Unfortunately, they do not report the tax rate. Based on evidence from other sources (Eichner and Sinai), the tax rate is probably around 25%. Using that tax rate, the coefficient is 1.126 and suggests an elasticity at a 22% rate of 0.25, very close to the Burman and Randolph results. They find a transitory elasticity of 4.9 (4.1% at a 22% rate).

Auerbach and Siegel also report an alternative specification in which they add several instruments to the permanent tax rate including the first dollar tax rate for the current year and the year ahead maximum statutory rate to a regression on the next year's tax rate. The permanent elasticity is much higher, 1.75 rather than 0.33. This magnitude of elasticity similar to that found in panel and cross-section studies in the 1 980s. The problem with their approach is that this addition of the current first dollar rate likely adds a transitory element to the permanent tax rate, which explains their significantly larger elasticity. Thus, the 1.126 coefficient is reported in **Table 1**.

Auerbach and Siegel also provide a separate regression for the very wealthy and for "sophisticated" taxpayers (who report sales of more complicated financial products such as derivatives or report short sales). Their findings using the Burman and Randolph methodology indicate that there is essentially no response for these taxpayers.

Eichner and Sinai (2000)

This study extends time series analysis through 1997, but finds that it is important to exclude 1986 from the estimates. When 1986 is excluded the coefficient is 2.28, for an elasticity of 0.5. There is also a case for excluding 1997, although it is not as important. When both are excluded, the coefficient in a semi-log specification is 2.18, which implies, at a 22% tax rate, an elasticity of 0.48. As in the case of Gillingham and Greenlees, many specifications are tried. One approach used an instrumental variables method relying on the top marginal tax rate. This approach led to an estimate of 3.8, for an elasticity of 0.84. Curiously, the coefficient changes quite substantially when 1997 was also excluded, to 5.13 and an elasticity of 1.13. One of the problems of using the top marginal tax rate is that differences between that tax rate and the average tax rate in the years before 1986 when the tax benefit was an exclusion and rates where more steeply graduated. The authors also tried some specifications with changes in tax rates. These tended to lead to elasticities ranging from 0.83 to 1.46. However, in most of these cases some or most of the tax rate coefficients were not statistically significant. Moreover, it is more likely that this approach reflects more transitory elements. Given the problems with using marginal rates and the instability of specifications with tax rate changes, the 2.28 coefficient is reported in **Table 1**.

Auten and Joulfaian (2004)

This analysis uses a longer micro-data panel (over 17 years) to estimate permanent and transitory effects. Although they include state tax rates, they do not use the state tax variation to identify permanent effects. Their approach is similar to the panel studies of the 1 980s in that it uses adjacent years to separate permanent and transitory effects. Their estimate is lower than most estimates of short panels from the 1980s, although this lower elasticity may reflect time series elements. It is likely, however, that the permanent estimate contains transitory elements. They find an elasticity of 0.72 at an apparent

20% tax rate, which indicates a coefficient of 3.6 and an elasticity of 0.79 at a 22% tax rate.

Evans (2009)

The Evans study is a basic cross-section regression, relying on the public use file, with a number of different specifications, leading to elasticities typically between 2 and 5. Although there are some issues associated with the public use file data, because tax returns are blended for high- income taxpayers to protect confidentiality, the main reservation about this study is that it reflects the fundamental, and now widely recognized, shortcomings of cross-section studies, and the findings cannot be interpreted as reflecting permanent realizations elasticities. These results are not reflected in **Table 1**.

APPENDIX C. CITATIONS TO STUDIES

Citations to Studies of the 1980s (in Table B-1)

Auerbach, Alan J. "Capital Gains Taxation and Tax Reform." *National Tax Journal* (September 1989), pp. 391-401.

Auten, Gerald E. "Capital Gains Taxes and Realizations: Can a Tax Cut Pay for Itself?" *Policy Studies Journal* (Autumn 1980), pp. 53-60.

Auten, Gerald E; Leonard E Burman; William C. Randolph. "Estimation and Interpretation of Capital Gains Realization Behavior: Evidence from Panel Data." *National Tax Journal* (September 1989), p. 353374. (This study was also released by the U.S. Department of Treasury. OTA Paper 67, May 1989).

Auten, Gerald E; Charles Clotfelter. "Permanent vs. Transitory Effects and the Realization of Capital Gains." *Quarterly Journal of Economics* (November 1982), pp. 613-632.

Congressional Budget Office. *Effects of the 1981 Act on the Distribution of Income and Taxes Paid.* Staff Working Paper. August 1986.

Congressional Budget Office. *How Capital Gains Tax Rates Affect Revenues: The Historical Evidence*. March 1988.

Darby, Michael; Robert Gillingham; John S. Greenlees. "The Direct Revenue Effects of Capital Gains Taxation: A Reconsideration of the Time Series Evidence." *Treasury Bulletin*, U.S. Department of Treasury. June 1988.

Feldstein, Martin; Joel Slemrod; Shlomo Yitzhaki. "The Effects of Taxation on the Selling of Corporate Stock and the Realization of Capital Gains." *Quarterly Journal of Economics* (June 1980), pp. 777-791.

Gillingham, Robert; John S. Greenlees; Kimberly D. Zieschang. *New Estimates of Capital Gains Realization Behavior: Evidence from Pooled Cross Section Data*. U. S. Department of Treasury, OTA Paper 66. May 1989.

Jones, Jonathan D. *An Analysis of Aggregate Time Series Capital Gains Equations*. U. S. Department of Treasury, Office of Tax Analysis Paper 65. May 1989.

Lindsey, Larry. *Capital Gains: Rates, Realizations, and Revenues*. National Bureau of Economic Research, Working Paper 1893. April, 1986.

Minarik, Joseph. "The Effects of Taxation on the Selling of Corporate Stock and the Realization of Capital Gains: Comment." *Quarterly Journal of Economics* (February 1984), pp. 93-110.

U.S. Department of Treasury. Office of Tax Analysis. *Report to the Congress on the Capital Gains Tax Reductions of 1978*. September 1985.

Citations to Studies Since the 1980s

[1] Auerbach, Alan J; Jonathan M. Siegel, "Capital-Gains Realizations of the Rich and Sophisticated," *American Economic Review*, Vol. 90, Papers and Proceedings of the 0ne Hundred Twelfth Annual Meeting of the American Economic Association, May 200, pp. 276-282.

Auten, Gerald; David Joulfaian, "*Taxes and Capital Gains Realizations: Evidence from a Long Panel*," Prepared for Presentation at the Society of Government Economists session at the Allied Social Science Association Meetings, January8, 2005, December 2004. Posted at http://www.aeaweb.org/annual_mtg_papers/2005/0109_0800_1204.pdf.

Bogart, William T; William M. Gentry, "Capital Gains Taxes and Realizations: Evidence from Interstate Comparisons." *Review of Economics and Statistics*, vol. 77 (May 1995), pp. 267-282.

Burman, Leonard E; William C. Randolph, "Measuring Permanent Responses to Capital Gains Tax Change in Panel Data," *American Economic Review*, vol. 83 (September 1994), pp. 794-809.

Evans, Paul. "The Relationship Between Realized Capital Gains and Their marginal Rate of Taxation, 1976-2004." October 9, 2009. Posted at http://iret.org/pub/CapitalGains-2.pdf.

Eichner, Matthew; Todd Sinai, "Capital Gains Tax Realizations and Tax Rates: New Evidence from Time Series." *National Tax Journal*, vol. 53, no.3, part 2 (September 2000), pp. 663-682.

Gillingham, Robert; John S. Greenlees, "The Effect of Marginal Tax Rates on Capital Gains Revenue: Another Look at the Evidence," *National Tax Journal*, vol. 45 (June 1992), pp. 167- 177.

Slemrod, Joel; William Shobe, *The Tax Elasticity of Capital Gains Realizations: Evidence from a Panel of Taxpayers*. National Bureau of Economic Research, Working Paper 3237. January 1990. Posted at http://www.nber.org/papers/w3237.pdf.

End Notes

[1] FY2019 is used as an example of a long run effect; the first few years may differ as a result of assumed short-term responses. In addition, later years may reflect more normal times as asset values are more likely to have rebounded fully from the recession. For the Treasury estimates, see *General Explanation of the Administration's FY2011 Revenue Proposals*, February 2010, p. 153, at http://www.treas.gov/offices/tax-policy

[2] This calculation is based on an average tax rate of 13.3% in 2008 and 17.9% in 2019 (supplied by CBO), with the differential applied to projected realizations in 2019, in Congressional Budget Office, *The Budget and Economic Outlook: Fiscal Years 2010 to 2020*, p. 85, at http://www.cbo.gov/ftpdocs/108xx/doc10871/01-26-Outlook.pdf.

[3] Numerous other issues are relevant to evaluation of capital gains taxes including economic effects and distributional concerns. See CRS Report R40411, *The Economic Effects of Capital Gains Taxation*, by Thomas L. Hungerford, and CRS Report 96-769, *Capital Gains Taxes: An Overview*, by Jane G. Gravelle.

[4] This treatment is called step-up in basis and means that when the heir sells an asset, the basis, or amount deducted from the sales price to determine taxable gain, will be the value at the time of death rather than the original acquisition cost of the decedent. This rule is temporarily suspended for 2010, although there is a $1.3 million exemption for gains created through this mechanism.

[5] This rule is not strictly applicable for large changes since the elasticity may change as the tax rate changes.

[6] Gains could fall a little more initially because the gains not realized today would be available in the future, and also because of sticker shock. But this phenomenon is very different from the large responses in gains that are from the current stock of gains with a tax cut. It is also a timing effect, but evidence suggests that, in the steady state, virtually all of the accrued gains not realized are never realized, but held until death. See Jane Gravelle, "Limits to Capital Gains Feedback Effects," *Tax Notes* 51, April 22, 1991, pp. 363-371.

[7] Supplied by the Congressional Budget Office.

[8] The shares of dividends and capital gains for these higher income taxes is based on data in the public use file provided by Maxim Shvedov, Analyst in Public Finance, Congressional Research Service.

[9] If affected taxpayers received approximately 50% of dividends, but only about 20% of the rate difference is applied, only about 13% of the total revenue from allowing dividend tax cuts to expire would be collected, as compared to 80% of the revenue from allowing capital gains tax cuts to expire.

[10] During that time, tax changes were constrained by deficit targets under legislation popularly known as Gramm- Rudman. See CRS Report RL30009, *Tax-Cut Legislation: Applicable Budget Enforcement Procedures*, by Robert Keith.

[11] Sources for these data are in an archived CRS report that was published in *Tax Notes*, Jane Gravelle, "Can A Capital Gains Tax Cut Pay for Itself?" *Tax Notes* 48, July 9, 1990, pp. 209-219. These elasticities are reported before adjustments for portfolio responses and are larger than the elasticities actually used for revenue estimating, which were 0.7 and approximately 0.9.

[12] The three panel studies, whose results are reported along with other studies in **Appendix B**, originally reported elasticities of 0.55, 1.29 and 1.65. This range was still wide, but the upper limit was much lower than the high estimates in cross-section studies. Moreover, the 0.55 may have been low because of the low tax rate in that study. As discussed in the next section, however, the elasticity for the latest panel study (Gerald E. Auten, Leonard E. Burman, and William C. Randolph, "Estimation and Interpretation of Capital Gains Realization Behavior: Evidence from Panel Data." *National Tax Journal*, September 1989, pp. 353-374.) was reported as 1.65, but should have been reported as 3.2. This estimate was similar to the estimates from single year cross sections. Thus the short-panel approach did not appear to address the transitory issue. The other micro-data approach, pooled cross-section times series, with a 1.18 elasticity, also likely reflects a mix of permanent and transitory effects.

[13] These data are reported in Robert Gillingham and John S. Greenlees, "The Effect of Marginal Tax Rates on Capital Gains Revenue: Another Look at the Evidence," *National Tax Journal*, vol. 45, June 1992, p. 176.

[14] See Leonard E. Burman, Kimberly A. Clausing, and John F. O'Hare, "Tax Reform and Realizations of Capital Gains in 1986," *National Tax Journal*, vol. 47, March 1994, pp. 1-18.

[15] All of these studies are summarized in **Appendix B**, but two are excluded because they basically repeat the now discredited methodologies of cross-section and short-panel studies.

[16] Coefficients currently used were provided by these agencies.

[17] For that reason, CBO does not focus as heavily on specification with respect to the tax rate as researchers concentrating on the realizations response might. For example, the CBO regression does not use instrumental variables. CBO also notes that the estimated realizations response is sensitive to other variables included. For other specifications, CBO finds a realization coefficient as large as 2.9.

[18] This study is an archived CRS report, which was published by Tax Notes. See Jane Gravelle, "Limits to Capital Gains Feedback Effects," *Tax Notes* 51, April 22, 1991, pp. 363-371.

[19] See, for example, Alan J. Auerbach, "Capital Gains Taxation and Tax Reform," *National Tax Journal*, September 1989, pp. 391-401.

[20] The study reported the elasticity of shares, rather than realizations. This point is discussed further in Jane Gravelle, "Limits to Capital Gains Feedback Effects," *Tax Notes* 51, April 22, 1991, pp. 363-371.

[21] Portfolio effects adjusted revenue effects from a capital gains tax to account for shifting investments out of capital gains producing assets taxed at a lower rate to other assets whose income would be taxed at higher rates.

[22] It was not possible in most cases to adjust the results for a consistent tax rate and the 0.55 panel estimate may reflect an unusually low tax rate. The 0.62 cross-section estimate may be affected by treatment of the truncation of gains at zero.

[23] These issues are discussed in Jane Gravelle "Can A Capital Gains Tax Cut Pay for Itself?" *Tax Notes* 48, July 9, 1990, pp. 209-219.

[24] With instrumental variables (which is done by a two-stage least squares method), a preliminary regression treats the tax rate as the dependent variable (endogenous) and estimates it using other predetermined instrurments. For example, one approach is to regress the actual tax rate on first dollar rate, predicted rate, maximum rate, etc. and use the fitted values in the

final regression, where the dependent variable is realizations. Using the maximum tax rate alone cannot be used in a single cross-section regression and it is problematic in time series studies that cover periods when the relationship between the maximum and average rate changed over time due to changes in the law.

[25] When a small coefficient is statistically insignificant, the data may be reliable but the confidence interval includes zero because it is a small effect. It may be reasonable to conclude that the effect is quite small, and perhaps nonexistent. When a large coefficient is not statistically significant, it suggests that there is a lot of uncertainty in the relationship and the result is not reliable.

In: Capital Gains Taxation
Editors: M. Zimmerman, L. Curtis ISBN: 978-1-62081-076-7

Chapter 4

TAX TREATMENT OF LONG-TERM CAPITAL GAINS AND DIVIDENDS AND RELATED PROVISIONS IN THE PRESIDENT'S FY2011 BUDGET PROPOSAL*

Maxim Shvedov

SUMMARY

Pending expiration at the end of 2010 of tax cuts enacted during the presidency of George W. Bush raises important questions about the future of affected tax policies. Tax treatment of longterm capital gains and dividends was one of the key components of the overall tax cut package. Long-term capital gains or losses arise from a sale or exchange of a capital asset, such as shares of stock, held for a year or longer by a taxpayer. Dividends are any distributions made by a corporation to its shareholders. This report discusses their tax treatment under current law and the President's FY2011 Budget Proposal, analyzes economic characteristics of affected taxpayers, and presents some policy alternatives with respect to this element of the tax system.

Historically capital gains and dividends were often treated differently from ordinary income, such as salaries and wages, and from each other. With the

---

* This is an edited, reformatted and augmented version of a Congressional Research Service Publication, CRS Report for Congress R41394, dated September 7, 2010.

passage of the Jobs and Growth Tax Relief Reconciliation Act of 2003 (JGTRRA, P.L. 108-27), long-term capital gains and qualified dividends were taxed at identical rates. In 2010 the rates are 15% or 0%, the latter if a taxpayer's marginal tax rate on ordinary income is 15% or lower. This treatment compares to the tax rates of 10% to 35% on ordinary income in 2010 (changing to 15% to 39.6% in 2011 under current law). If tax reductions first enacted under JGTRRA are allowed to expire, long-term capital gains would become subject to 20% or 10% rate and dividends would be treated as ordinary income and subject to ordinary tax rates.

Compared to current law, the President's FY2011 Budget Proposal would reduce the tax rates on capital gains in 2011 and thereafter for taxpayers below certain income thresholds, and on dividends for taxpayers at all income levels. In addition, it would sustain the parity in tax treatment of both types of income. The Administration proposes to retain the 0%/15% rate structure for both capital gains and dividends after 2010 for married taxpayers with income below $250,000 and non-married taxpayers with income under $200,000 (together referred to as FY2011 income threshold). Taxpayers above the threshold would be subject to a 20% rate on both kinds of income. Relative to current law, the President's proposal is estimated to reduce revenues by $238.3 billion over 10 years.

Economic characteristics of the recipients of these types of income play an important role in analyzing the policy. By value, long-term dividends and particularly capital gains are disproportionately distributed among a relatively small number of higher income returns. By numbers, returns with income below $200,000 represent a majority of recipients for both kinds of income, but a minority within their respective income classes.

Based on the analysis of IRS data, the largest shares of capital gains and dividends by value would be subject to the 20% rate if President's proposal were enacted. The second largest share would be exempt from tax, due to a 0% rate. Long-term capital gains and qualified dividends subject to a 15% tax would represent the smallest share. Only 5% of the long-term capital gains and 14% of dividends would be subject to the 15% rate. Thus, the third 15% bracket materially affects a modest number of taxpayers, but makes the tax structure more complex for all taxpayers.

The report concludes with analysis of several legislative options. Besides across-the-board extension or expiration of the tax cuts, some other options may achieve some of the desired distributional goals without adding to the code the complexity of a three-tiered tax rate structure.

The pending expiration, at the end of 2010, of the tax cuts enacted in the past decade raises important questions about the future of these tax policies. Policymakers' proposals range from the indefinite extension of the cuts for all taxpayers to allowing them to expire without any action.

This report focuses on one of the key components of the expiring tax cut package, the treatment of long-term capital gains and qualified dividends. It discusses current law, analyzes economic characteristics of affected taxpayers, and presents some policy alternatives with respect to this element of the tax system.

CAPITAL GAINS, DIVIDENDS, AND THEIR TAX TREATMENT

Capital gains or losses arise from a sale or exchange of a capital asset by a taxpayer. In general, any property is a "capital asset," except for specific classes excluded by the tax code. In addition, the tax code differentiates among separate classes of capital assets, such as stocks, real estate, livestock, or collectibles. Tax treatment of capital gains and losses differs across asset classes.

Capital gains income may be subject to a special set of tax rates, which are lower than the tax rates applicable to other kinds of income, such as salaries or interest (referred to below as ordinary income). This report discusses the treatment of long-term capital gains, which are defined under the tax code as gains from sales of assets held for more than a year. These rates apply, for example, to gains from the sales of stocks and bonds.

The capital gains rate structure effective in 2010 was first adopted by the Jobs and Growth Tax Relief Reconciliation Act of 2003 (JGTRRA, P.L. 108-27) and later extended by Tax Increase Prevention and Reconciliation Act of 2005 (TIPRA, P.L. 109-222). Under current law long-term capital gains are taxed at 15% in 2010, or, if taxpayer's marginal tax rate on ordinary income is 15% or lower, capital gains are taxed at 0%. This treatment compares to the statutory marginal tax rates of 10% to 35% on ordinary income in 2010. The capital gains rates in fact set the maximum rate applicable to this kind of income. So, if taxpayer's marginal tax rate on ordinary income is below the capital gains tax rate, the lower rate would apply. Short-term capital gains are taxed at ordinary-income tax rates.

Under current law the structure of the long-term capital gains tax rates is set to change in 2011 with the expiration of TIPRA's provisions. The most important aspect of the change, as far as long-term capital gains are concerned, would be an increase in the tax rates from 15% to 20% and from 0% to 10%. There would also be some slightly lower rates (8% and 18%) for assets held for five years or more.[1] The personal tax rates on ordinary income would also change under current law, ranging from 15% to 39.6% in 2011 and thereafter.

Another income item recognized by the tax code is dividends, which are any distribution made by a corporation to its shareholders. Dividends are subject to ordinary tax rates, but dividends received from domestic corporations and qualified foreign corporations ("qualified dividends") are currently subject to the long-term capital gains tax rates under current law.

These lower rates for qualified dividends were also introduced by JGTRRA in 2003. TIPRA extended this preferential treatment of qualified dividends through the end of 2010. Historically, the treatment of dividends under the individual income tax varied greatly.[2] Immediately prior to the JGTRRA's enactment all dividends were taxed as ordinary income.

In 2011, under current law, however, tax treatment of dividends would revert back to ordinary income. As a result, in 2011 dividend income would become subject once again to the ordinary tax rates, which would vary from 15% to 39.6%.[3] Even though the lowest statutory marginal tax rate would be 15% in 2011, for a large number of lower- and middle-income taxpayers the effective marginal tax rate on ordinary income, including dividends, would be 0% due to a variety of deductions and credits.[4]

This pending change would not only increase the tax rates applicable to the dividend income, but also reintroduce a difference in the tax treatment of capital gains and dividends. Generally speaking, selling stock shares or receiving dividends are alternate ways by which shareholders receive the proceeds from their investment. A difference in their tax treatment would make dividends disadvantageous to the shareholders from the tax perspective.[5]

Taxpayers who receive income from capital gains and dividends generally fill out Schedule D of IRS Form 1040, the standard form for individual income tax filing. This schedule is considered one of the more difficult forms to fill out. For example, IRS estimated that it took 27.5 hours to complete and file an average tax return that required Schedules A (itemized deductions schedule) and D, compared to 13.7 hours required to file an average return without these two schedules.[6]

Finally, this report does not discuss tax treatment of investment income received through individual retirement arrangements (IRAs) and other similar tax-preferred plans. These plans are subject to a separate set of tax rules. This report discusses the issues affecting only the regular investment income.

THE PRESIDENT'S FY2011 BUDGET PROPOSAL

Compared to current law, the President's FY2011 Budget Proposal would reduce the tax rates on capital gains in 2011 and thereafter for taxpayers below certain income thresholds, and on dividends for taxpayers at all income levels. In addition, it would sustain the parity in tax treatment of both types of income. In its FY2011 budget submission, the Administration proposes to retain the 0%/1 5% rate structure for both capital gains and dividends after 2010 for married taxpayers with income below $250,000 and non-married taxpayers with income under $200,000 (together identified below as FY2011 income threshold). Taxpayers above the threshold would be subject to a 20% rate on both kinds of income. The Joint Committee on Taxation estimated the cost of this provision at $238.3 billion over FY2010 - FY2020.[7]

This proposal reflects the President's pledge not to increase taxes on taxpayers below this income threshold. Broadly speaking, this commitment is intended to make the overall tax system more progressive. A tax system is called "progressive" when the tax burden, represented as a share of income, increases with income.

Under the Administration proposal, taxpayers with income above the FY20 11 income threshold would be subject to a 20% tax rate on capital gains. According to the explanation of the proposal from the Treasury, this set of higher rates would apply "for married taxpayers filing jointly with income over $250,000 less the standard deduction and two personal exemptions (indexed from 2009) and for single taxpayers with income over $200,000 less the standard deduction and one personal exemption (indexed from 2009)."[8] Thus, the Administration would essentially revert to the pre-JGTRRA treatment of capital gains for higher-income taxpayers. Taxpayers below the FY2011 income threshold would continue to be subject to lower, or even no (in case of a 0% rate), capital gains taxes.

At the same time, the Administration proposes to continue to subject qualified dividends to the long-term capital gains rates. This would represent a tax cut for taxpayers at all levels of income, even if capital gains rates increase to 20%. This higher rate is still lower than the tax rates on ordinary income for higher-income taxpayers. For example, taxpayers above the FY2011 income threshold would be subject to 31%, 36%, or 39.6% tax rate on ordinary income in 2011 under current law. In a fairly uncommon situation of taxpayer's marginal tax rate on ordinary income being below the capital gains tax rate, the lower of the two rates would apply.

On April 22, 2010, the Senate Budget Committee approved a FY2011 budget resolution, which assumes extension of the middle-class tax relief estimated to cost $780 billion over five years. The measure accommodates the extension of a number of tax relief provisions enacted during the past decade limited to taxpayers with income below $200,000 or $250,000, depending on filing status.[9] The measure accommodates an extension of the capital gains tax cuts in a vein similar to the President's proposal, but it is unclear whether the revenue targets specified in the resolution would allow for dividend tax relief.[10]

A number of bills related to the taxation of capital gains and dividends have been introduced in the 111th Congress.[11] So far none of them has seen action. Press reports indicate that congressional activity on the issue, as well as other tax cuts enacted in 2000s, may occur later this year.

Economic Characteristics of Taxpayers Receiving Capital Gains and Dividends

In order to understand the distributional implications of possible capital gains and dividends tax policy changes, it may be useful to analyze the economic profile of taxpayers receiving long-term capital gains and dividend income. Both of these income items are distributed unevenly across taxpayers with different income. Thus changes in the law would have different economic consequences for different groups of taxpayers.

The following distributional conclusions are illustrated using the data for 2006, the latest tax year for which data are available at the necessary level of detail. It is expected that the specifics will change from year to year, but the broad distributional conclusions are robust with respect to normal fluctuations in economic variables.

Long-Term Capital Gains

Table 1 shows the distribution of long-term capital gains and their recipients across the income spectrum. It shows how total capital gains are distributed across income classes as measured by adjusted gross income (AGI). AGI is a broad measure of income used in the tax code.[12]

Table 2 shows the distribution of the long-term capital gains within each income class. It shows how many taxpayers within each income class received long-term capital gains. It also shows that on aggregate approximately 13% of returns nationwide claimed this kind of income.

Several characteristics of the distribution of the long-term capital gains across the income spectrum become apparent from **Table 1** and **Table 2**:

1. By number of returns, the majority of taxpayers claiming capital gains are lower- and middle-income taxpayers. Approximately 85% of all taxpayers claiming long-term capital gains income have AGI below $200,000. At the same time, taxpayers with AGI below $200,000 represent 97% of all returns. Thus, a less than proportional share of lower- and middle-income taxpayers received longterm capital gains income.
2. Even though the number of these taxpayers is large in absolute terms, they represent a minority in their respective income classes. The share of returns claiming capital gains varies from 5.6% to 33.4% for income classes below $200,000. In contrast, the shares vary from 59.6% to 96.9% for income classes with AGI above $200,000.
3. By value, the share of all long-term capital gains attributable to taxpayers with lower and middle income is small. Taken together, taxpayers with income below $200,000 claimed approximately 16% of all long-term capital gains. Within that group, income classes with AGI below $100,000 receive an insignificant share of the total capital gains—for none of them the share is above 2.7% of the total long-term capital gains. Taxpayers with AGI between $100,000 and $200,000 receive less than 10% of the total long-term capital gains income.
4. Higher-income taxpayers, about 15% of all returns with long-term capital gains, claim most of the capital gains by value (nearly 84%). The top income class of taxpayers with AGI in excess of $10 million received over 26% of all capital gains in 2006, but accounted for just 0.08% (rounded up to 0.1% in **Table 1**) of all returns claiming this kind of income.

   While some higher income classes, such as the one between $1.5 million and $2 million, appear to receive a small share of the total

(4.3%), it is important to keep in mind that there are relatively few taxpayers in this class—only about 56,000. Compare this to any of the income classes below $100,000, which account for millions of returns each, but receive a considerably smaller share of the total long-term capital gains (the highest share is 2.7%).

5. The recipients of the long-term capital gains represent a majority in the higher income classes. Over a half of taxpayers in each of the income classes over $200,000 received long-term capital gains in 2006. For the top income class, almost 97% did so.

Table 1. Distribution of Long-Term Capital Gains (LTCG) by Income, 2006

Income		LTCG, million dollars	Share of the Total LTCG	Returns with LTCG	Share of All Returns with LTCG
from	to				
	$10,000	$10,502.4	1.5%	1,833,691	10.1%
$10,000	$20,000	$2,200.8	0.3%	1,283,810	7.1%
$20,000	$30,000	$3,301.7	0.5%	1,074,730	5.9%
$30,000	$40,000	($3,428.8)	-0.5%	1,034,394	5.7%
$40,000	$50,000	$4,213.7	0.6%	1,123,720	6.2%
$50,000	$75,000	$15,686.4	2.2%	2,811,424	15.5%
$75,000	$100,000	$18,792.2	2.7%	2,294,848	12.7%
$100,000	$200,000	$64,062.8	9.1%	4,019,911	22.2%
$200,000	$500,000	$98,006.7	13.8%	1,866,272	10.3%
$500,000	$1,000,000	$75,412.6	10.7%	469,815	2.6%
$1,000,000	$1,500,000	$43,380.8	6.1%	129,458	0.7%
$1,500,000	$2,000,000	$30,249.3	4.3%	56,272	0.3%
$2,000,000	$5,000,000	$90,788.3	12.8%	89,301	0.5%
$5,000,000	$10,000,000	$68,020.0	9.6%	23,571	0.1%
$10,000,000		$187,054.5	26.4%	15,231	0.1%
Total		$708,243.3	100.0%	18,126,448	100.0%

Source: CRS calculations based on IRS Public Use Tax File data.

Notes: Negative dollar amounts mean net capital losses (losses exceeding gains). Data include returns with negative AGI.

Table 2. Share of Returns with Long-Term Capital Gains (LTCG) Within Each Income Class, 2006

Income		Returns with LTCG	All Returns	Share of Returns with LTCG
from	to			
	$10,000	1,833,691	25,958,575	7.1%
$10,000	$20,000	1,283,810	22,770,197	5.6%
$20,000	$30,000	1,074,730	18,400,562	5.8%
$30,000	$40,000	1,034,394	13,978,335	7.4%
$40,000	$50,000	1,123,720	10,610,656	10.6%
$50,000	$75,000	2,811,424	18,993,164	14.8%
$75,000	$100,000	2,294,848	11,143,297	20.6%
$100,000	$200,000	4,019,911	12,049,372	3 3.4%
$200,000	$500,000	1,866,272	3,133,137	59.6%
$500,000	$1,000,000	469,815	591,166	79.5%
$1,000,000	$1,500,000	129,458	149,592	86.5%
$1,500,000	$2,000,000	56,272	63,587	88.5%
$2,000,000	$5,000,000	89,301	99,653	89.6%
$5,000,000	$10,000,000	23,571	24,927	94.6%
$10,000,000		15,231	15,727	96.9%
Total		18,126,448	137,981,947	13.1%

Source: CRS calculations based on IRS Public Use Tax File data.

Qualified Dividends

Table 3 and **Table 4** provide information about the recipients of qualified dividend income analogous to that presented in **Table 1** and **Table 2**.[13] Generally speaking, dividends are also distributed unevenly, exhibiting a pattern that shares many common features with the pattern of capital gains distribution.

However, qualified dividends are less concentrated in the higher income classes than long-term capital gains.

Table 3. Distribution of Qualified Dividends (QD) by Income, 2006

Income		Qualified Dividends, million dollars	Share of the Total QD	Returns with QD	Share of All Returns with QD
from	to				
	$10,000	$2,414.5	1.8%	2,702,045	10.3%
$10,000	$20,000	$2,122.4	1.6%	2,091,139	8.0%
$20,000	$30,000	$2,279.4	1.7%	1,691,653	6.4%
$30,000	$40,000	$2,181.8	1.6%	1,673,059	6.4%
$40,000	$50,000	$2,902.3	2.1%	1,814,636	6.9%
$50,000	$75,000	$8,276.2	6.1%	4,354,842	16.6%
$75,000	$100,000	$9,147.8	6.7%	3,433,508	13.1%
$100,000	$200,000	$22,236.1	16.3%	5,591,649	21.3%
$200,000	$500,000	$21,954.7	16.1%	2,138,453	8.1%
$500,000	$1,000,000	$12,584.0	9.3%	482,576	1.8%
$1,000,000	$1,500,000	$6,563.8	4.8%	128,082	0.5%
$1,500,000	$2,000,000	$3,979.9	2.9%	55,314	0.2%
$2,000,000	$5,000,000	$11,525.1	8.5%	86,339	0.3%
$5,000,000	$10,000,000	$6,872.4	5.1%	22,818	0.1%
$10,000,000		$21,033.2	15.5%	14,776	0.1%
Total		$136,073.7	100.0%	26,280,889	100.0%

Source: CRS calculations based on IRS Public Use Tax File data.

Table 4 shows the distribution of the qualified dividends within each income class. It shows how many taxpayers within each income class received qualified dividends.

It also shows that on aggregate approximately 19% of returns nationwide claimed this kind of income.

There is a great deal of similarity between the economic characteristics of the recipients of dividends and long-term capital gains. In fact, most of the broad observations listed in the previous section can be repeated here. Dividend income is disproportionately distributed among a relatively small number of higher income returns. Returns with income below $200,000 represent a majority of recipients by numbers, but the minority within their respective income classes.

At the same time, the distribution of dividend income is not as uneven as that of the long-term capital gains. To illustrate this point, **Table 5** reproduces selected data from **Table 1** through **Table 4**.

Table 4. Share of Returns with Qualified Dividends (QD) within Each Income Class, 2006

Income, from	Income, up to	Returns with QD	All Returns	Share of Returns with QD
	$10,000	2,702,045	25,958,575	10.4%
$10,000	$20,000	2,091,139	22,770,197	9.2%
$20,000	$30,000	1,691,653	18,400,562	9.2%
$30,000	$40,000	1,673,059	13,978,335	12.0%
$40,000	$50,000	1,814,636	10,610,656	17.1%
$50,000	$75,000	4,354,842	18,993,164	22.9%
$75,000	$100,000	3,433,508	11,143,297	30.8%
$100,000	$200,000	5,591,649	12,049,372	46.4%
$200,000	$500,000	2,138,453	3,133,137	68.3%
$500,000	$1,000,000	482,576	591,166	81.6%
$1,000,000	$1,500,000	128,082	149,592	85.6%
$1,500,000	$2,000,000	55,314	63,587	87.0%
$2,000,000	$5,000,000	86,339	99,653	86.6%
$5,000,000	$10,000,000	22,818	24,927	91.5%
$10,000,000		14,776	15,727	94.0%
Total		26,280,889	137,981,947	19.1%

Source: CRS calculations based on IRS Public Use Tax File data.

Comparing respective shares in **Table 5**, every income class below $200,000 receives a larger share of total dividend income than that of total long-term capital gains. For example, taxpayers with income between $50,000 and $75,000 receive 6.1% of total dividends, but only 2.2% of the long-term capital gains.

The reverse is true about most higher income classes. For example, the top income class received 15.5% of all dividends, but 26.4% of all long-term capital gains.

The distribution of returns with dividends is also somewhat more even than that of the long-term capital gains. For example, taxpayers with AGI between $50,000 and $75,000 represent 16.6% of all returns claiming dividend income, but 15.5% of returns with long-term capital gains. In that income class, 22.9% of taxpayers received dividends, but only 14.8% received long-term capital gains. The relationship reverses for income classes above $1 million.

Distribution Relative to FY2011 Income Threshold

The President's proposal would apply a different structure of tax rates on long-term capital gains and dividends to taxpayers below and above the FY20 11 budget income threshold, defined as $250,000 for married taxpayers and $200,000 for all others. Given this proposal, it may be helpful to analyze distributions relative to this threshold.

Under the President's proposal, some taxpayers below the FY2011 income threshold would be eligible for 0% rate on this type of income, while others would pay the tax at 15% rate. Taxpayers with taxable income subject to 15% or lower statutory marginal tax rate on ordinary income are eligible for 0% rate on long-term capital gains and qualified dividends. Taxable income, by definition, is equal to AGI minus deductions and exemptions. For example, in 2010, in order to qualify for 0% treatment, taxable income of married taxpayers cannot exceed $68,000. For a single taxpayer it must be below $34,000.

Table 5. Comparative Distribution of Long-Term Capital Gains (LTCG) and Qualified Dividends (QD), 2006

Income		Share of the Total Amount		Share of Returns		Share of Returns within Income Class	
from	to	LTCG	QD	LTCG	QD	LTCG	QD
	$10,000	1.5%	1.8%	10.1%	10.3%	7.1%	10.4%
$10,000	$20,000	0.3%	1.6%	7.1%	8.0%	5.6%	9.2%
$20,000	$30,000	0.5%	1.7%	5.9%	6.4%	5.8%	9.2%
$30,000	$40,000	-0.5%	1.6%	5.7%	6.4%	7.4%	12.0%
$40,000	$50,000	0.6%	2.1%	6.2%	6.9%	10.6%	17.1%
$50,000	$75,000	2.2%	6.1%	15.5%	16.6%	14.8%	22.9%
$75,000	$100,000	2.7%	6.7%	12.7%	13.1%	20.6%	30.8%
$100,000	$200,000	9.1%	16.3%	22.2%	21.3%	33.4%	46.4%
$200,000	$500,000	13.8%	16.1%	10.3%	8.1%	59.6%	68.3%
$500,000	$1,000,000	10.7%	9.3%	2.6%	1.8%	79.5%	81.6%
$1,000,000	$1,500,000	6.1%	4.8%	0.7%	0.5%	86.5%	85.6%
$1,500,000	$2,000,000	4.3%	2.9%	0.3%	0.2%	88.5%	87.0%
$2,000,000	$5,000,000	12.8%	8.5%	0.5%	0.3%	89.6%	86.6%
$5,000,000	$10,000,000	9.6%	5.1%	0.1%	0.1%	94.6%	91.5%
$10,000,000		26.4%	15.5%	0.1%	0.1%	96.9%	94.0%
Total		100.0%	100.0%	100.0%	100.0%	13.1%	19.1%

Source: CRS calculations based on IRS Public Use Tax File data.

Table 6. Distribution of Long-Term Capital Gains (LTCG) and Qualified Dividends (QD) by Their Treatment in the President's FY2011 Budget Proposal, 2006

Marginal Tax Rate on Ordinary Income (Proposed Rate on LTCG and QD)	Amounts, million dollars		Returns, millions		
	LTCG	QD	LTCG	QD	All
15% and below, under the FY2011 income threshold (Proposed 0% rate)	85,399.4	34,420.4	10.2	14.9	108.1
Above 15%, under the FY2011 income threshold (Proposed 15% rate)	35,039.8	18,483.3	5.5	8.8	26.2
Above the FY2011 income threshold (Proposed 20% rate)	587,804.1	83,170.0	2.4	2.6	3.6
Totals	708,243.3	136,073.7	18.1	26.3	138.0

Source: CRS calculations based on IRS Public Use Tax File data.

Hence, under the President's proposal one can distinguish three groups of taxpayers, depending on the way their long-term capital gains and dividend income would be taxed. The first group consists of taxpayers under the FY2011 income threshold eligible for 0% treatment. Second is the group below the FY2011 income threshold, to whom the 15% rate would apply. The third group contains taxpayers above the FY2011 income threshold, for whom the applicable tax rate on longterm capital gains and dividends would be 20%. **Table 6** provides statistics for each of these three groups.

Table 7 reproduces the same data as shares of the total for each column.

As can be seen from **Table 7**, the largest shares of capital gains (83%) and dividends (6 1%) by value would be subject to the 20% rate. The second largest share would be exempt from tax, due to a 0% rate.

Long-term capital gains and qualified dividends subject to a 15% tax would represent the smallest share. Only 5% of the long-term capital gains and 14% of dividends would be subject to the 15% rate.

In terms of the numbers of affected taxpayers the sizes of the three groups steadily decrease. This fact is largely determined by the uneven total number of taxpayers in each of the three groups. As **Table 6** shows, the lowest income group accounts for over 108 million returns, the second group—for over 26 million, and the highest income group—for less than 4 million returns. Thus the number of affected taxpayers decreases from one group to the next merely because the total number of returns decreases by a lot.

Tax Relief for Taxpayers Above the FY2011 Income Threshold

The President's proposal to extend the tax cuts for dividends benefits taxpayers across all income levels. The dividend proposal would reduce taxes relative to current law for taxpayers above the FY2011 income threshold of $200,000 or $250,000, as well as below it.

Table 8 shows the distribution of dividends by marginal tax rate and in relation to the FY2011 income threshold. Under the President's proposal, the top two individual marginal tax rates would change from 33% and 35% to 36% and 39.6% respectively. This means, for example, that taxpayers in the top bracket would pay approximately $8.5 billion less in taxes because of the change (= $35 billion multiplied by the difference between 39.6% and 20%). Accounting for economic growth and other factors, the impact of the provision would likely exceed $10 billion per year by 2012-2013, when transitionary effects are likely to subside.[14]

Table 7. Shares of Long-Term Capital Gains (LTCG) and Qualified Dividends (QD) by Their Treatment in the President's FY2011 Budget Proposal, 2006

Marginal Tax Rate on Ordinary Income (Proposed Rate on LTCG and QD)	Amounts		Returns		
	LTCG	QD	LTCG	QD	All
	Shares of the total				
MTR 15pct and below, under the FY2011 threshold (Proposed 0% rate)	12%	25%	56%	57%	78%
MTR above 15 pct, under the FY2011 threshold (Proposed 15% rate)	5%	14%	31%	33%	19%
Above the FY2011 threshold (Proposed 20% rate)	83%	61%	13%	10%	3%

Source: CRS calculations based on IRS Public Use Tax File data.

Table 8. Distribution of Dividends by Taxpayer's Marginal Tax Rate and Relative to the President's FY2011 Budget Proposal Income Threshold

Marginal tax rate	Qualified dividends, million dollars	
	Above FY2011 Threshold	Below FY2011 Threshold
0%	617	3,896
5%	127	3,976
10%	6	4,127
15%	24,145	22,422
25%	6,255	14,554
28%	7,110	3,897
33%	9,814	32
35%	35,095	-

Source: CRS calculations based on IRS Public Use Tax File data.

POLICY OPTIONS

Among the options available to policymakers with respect to tax treatment of capital gains and dividends are the following:

1. **Continue current law without a change.** Under this option the JGTRRA tax cuts would be allowed to expire. The long-term capital gains would increase to 10% or 20% depending on a taxpayer's income. Dividends would be treated as ordinary income and subject to the statutory rates of 15% to 39.6%.
   This option, by definition, would have no fiscal impact relative to current law. It would increase taxes compared to the 2010 tax structure on taxpayers below the FY2011 income threshold, as well as above it. It would maintain a two-tiered structure of the tax on capital gains. It would also reestablish the discrepancy in tax treatment between capital gains and dividends.
2. **Permanently extend JGTRRA tax cuts.** Under this option, the tax rate structure in effect in 2010 would remain effective indefinitely. The rates applied to capital gains would be 0% or 15%, depending on the taxpayer's income. Dividends would be subject to these rates, rather than to the rates applicable to the ordinary income.

This option would have a very large negative revenue impact.[15] It would maintain tax relief for taxpayers both below and above the FY2011 income threshold. It would maintain a two-tier structure of the tax rates on capital gains and dividends. It would also maintain the parity between the treatment of both types of income.

3. **Modify the rate structure as proposed by the President.** This option maintains lower rates for taxpayers below the income threshold from the President's FY2011 Budget Proposal. It would create a three-tiered tax rate structure of 0%, 15%, or 20%, depending on taxpayer's income. According to JCT and CBO, the cost of this option would be $238.3 billion relative to current law over ten years.[16]

   The revenue impact of this option is still quite high, even though it is considerably lower than the impact of across-the-board extension of the JGTRRA tax cuts. It would maintain tax relief for taxpayers below the FY2011 income threshold. The option would maintain the parity between the tax treatment of capital gains and dividends.

   At the same time, the proposal would complicate the tax structure, because it would create a three-tiered capital gains tax rate structure. Even though the newly created 15% bracket would apply to a small number of taxpayers, tax preparation would become more complex for all taxpayers. This effect raises a question about desirability of this approach. It might be possible, perhaps, to achieve similar distributional results without introducing new additional complexity into the tax system.

4. **Exempt a share of capital gains and dividends from taxation and tax the rest as ordinary income.** This alternative may provide lower tax rates on long-term capital gains and qualified dividends by exempting a share of capital gains and dividends from taxation. This approach would maintain progressivity of this element of the tax system, while making it computationally simpler. It would affect some taxpayers both below and above FY2011 income thresholds, although for most taxpayers below the threshold increase or decrease in tax liability would be small.

   Under this option, taxpayers would calculate their long-term capital gains and dividends in the same way they do it today, reduce these amounts by the amount of an exemption, and use the result in further tax calculations as an ordinary income item. This approach avoids the complication of filling out a special worksheet of Schedule D that helps determine which tax rate applies to which portion of taxable income. Currently, completing this worksheet may involve switching several times between Form 1040, Schedule D, and several worksheets in the instructions to these forms.

In economic terms this approach would be equivalent to applying marginal tax rates to capital income that are proportionately lower than the rates applicable to ordinary income. **Table 9** illustrates this concept for several hypothetical exemption shares, ranging from 20% to 50%.

For example, exempting 35% of capital income from the tax is equivalent to applying a 6.5% tax rate on capital income for taxpayers in a 10% ordinary income bracket, or 25.7% to taxpayers in 39.6% ordinary tax rate bracket. As can be seen from **Table A-1** in the **Appendix**, these values largely fall within a range of historic values of the rates on this type of income.

5. **Eliminate the 15% bracket and increase the upper bound of the 0% bracket.** This option may be tailored to simplify the structure of the capital gains rates in a revenue-neutral way. This change would benefit some taxpayers who would have been subject to the 15% rate, but receive an exemption instead due to the expansion of the 0% bracket. On the other hand some taxpayers, who would have been subject to 15% would become subject to the 20% rate. The reduced taxes of the first group would be offset by the increased liability of the second group.

   Compared to the President's proposal, the affected taxpayers would be confined to the "15% group": taxpayers who would have been eligible for the 15% rate on the long-term capital gains and dividends under the President's proposal. As **Table 6** and **Table 7** show, this is a small group of taxpayers by number and by the amount of capital income involved. While, technically speaking, this change would result in an increase in tax liability for some taxpayers below the FY2011 income threshold, such an increase would be offset by the decrease to other taxpayers. At the same time, all taxpayers would benefit from a simpler tax system.

6. **Apply a 20% rate across the board, but expand tax-preferred investment accounts.** It is possible to apply a 20% tax rate to all long-term capital gains and dividends and use the additional revenues to expand or make less restrictive individual retirement accounts (IRAs), saver's credit, and other arrangements in the tax code that significantly reduce taxes applicable to capital income.

Table 9. Effective Tax Rates on Exempt Income under Several Assumptions about Hypothetical Exemption Percentages

Exemption:	20%	30%	35%	50%
Marginal Tax Rate on Ordinary Income	Effective Tax Rate on Exempt Income			
10%	8.0%	7.0%	6.5%	5.0%
15%	12.0%	10.5%	9.8%	7.5%
25%	20.0%	17.5%	16.3%	12.5%
28%	22.4%	19.6%	18.2%	14.0%
36%	28.8%	25.2%	23.4%	18.0%
39.6%	31.7%	27.7%	25.7%	19.8%

Source: CRS calculations based on IRS Public Use Tax File data.

This change may be beneficial in several ways. It would encourage lower-income investors to take advantage of tax-preferred investment mechanisms. It would also simplify the tax system. First, only one rate would apply to capital gains and dividends across the whole income spectrum. Second, if investors switch to long-term investing through IRAs, they would not have to deal with the complexities of reporting their capital income on an annual basis. Third, reducing restrictions would make IRAs and other arrangements simpler.

While, technically speaking, this change would result in an increase in tax liability for some taxpayers below the FY2011 income threshold, this structure of tax benefits may be more meaningful for lower- and middle-income investors. These investors do not benefit much from a 0% rate on capital income, because they do not have much of this kind of income in the first place. Even if they start investing and receiving capital gains and dividends, the amounts of tax savings are unlikely to become meaningful over shorter time horizons. Lack of constraints on withdrawals in the regular investment accounts and higher likelihood of emergency withdrawals would further hamper investment returns and reduce associated tax benefits for this group of taxpayers. On the other hand, longer term investing may yield non-trivial gains for them.

7. **Temporary extension.** Finally, all of the above options may be considered on a temporary basis. Given current budgetary and economic environment, it may be difficult to find a policy alternative that would adequately meet both long-term and short-term challenges.

Measures that ultimately result in an increase in the tax burden, might be undesirable when the economy is weak. On the other hand, measures that indefinitely reduce federal revenues would increase budget deficits, which is another issue of concern for policymakers. Thus, a compromise solution might involve combination of several policies, which would reduce the tax burden in the near future, but maintain the future revenue stream at the level comparable to current law in the later years, when the economy improves.

At the same time, some argue that contractionary effects of increased tax burden on higher-income taxpayers may be low, because these taxpayers typically do not change consumption by much when their disposable (after-tax) income fluctuates. The purpose of the stimulative fiscal policy, however, is to spur consumption in the short run. Thus, from the standpoint of the fast-acting economic stimulus, the argument goes, it may be better to channel any tax relief towards lower-income taxpayers, who are more likely to use any additional disposable income for immediate consumption.

Appendix. Long-Term Capital Gains and Taxes Paid on Long-Term Capital Gains

Table A-1. Long-Term Capital Gains and Taxes Paid on Long-Term Capital Gains, 1977-2007

(dollar amounts in millions)					
Year	**Realized Long-Term Capital Gains**	**Taxes Paid on Long-Term Capital Gains**	**Average Effective Tax Rate (percent)**	**Realized Gain as a Percent of GDP**	**Maximum Tax Rate on Long-Term Gains**
1977	43,755	7,870	18	1.57	39.875
1979	70,493	10,405	14.8	2.25	28
1980	69,856	10,817	15.5	2.23	28
1981	77,071	11,934	15.5	2.37	28.00/20.00
1982	86,087	12,500	14.5	2.65	20
1983	116,015	17,134	14.8	3.28	20
1984	135,936	20,365	15	3.46	20
1985	166,356	25,178	15.1	3.94	20

Table A-1. (Continued)

(dollar amounts in millions)					
Year	**Realized Long-Term Capital Gains**	**Taxes Paid on Long-Term Capital Gains**	**Average Effective Tax Rate (percent)**	**Realized Gain as a Percent of GDP**	**Maximum Tax Rate on Long-Term Gains**
1986	318,944	50,834	15.9	7.15	20
1987	140,386	31,791	22.6	2.96	28
1988	153,271	36,746	24	3.01	28
1989	141,069	32,351	22.9	2.57	28
1990	115,671	25,900	22.4	1.99	28
1991	98,363	21,581	21.9	1.64	28.93
1992	114,060	25,847	22.7	1.8	28.93
1993	134,469	31,393	23.3	2.02	29.19
1994	140,392	33,092	23.6	1.98	29.19
1995	158,955	38,368	24.1	2.14	29.19
1996	233,872	58,782	25.1	2.98	29.19
1997	330,360	69,572	21.1	3.96	29.19/2 1.19
1998	424,762	80,611	19	4.83	21.19
1999	482,181	91,416	19	5.16	21.19
2000	588,061	111,507	19	5.91	21.19
2001	322,831	58,750	18.2	3.14	21.17
2002	251,301	44,984	17.9	2.36	21.16
2003	294,811	44,903	15.2	2.65	2 1.05/16.05
2004	466,224	66,154	14.2	3.93	16.05
2005	648,430	92,304	14.2	5.13	16.05
2006	750,771	106,568	14.2	5.6	15.7
2007 (prelim)	861,220	121,933	14.2	6.12	15.7

Source: Department of the Treasury, Office of Tax Analysis, available at http://www.treas.gov/offices/tax-policy/ library/capgain2-2010.pdf.

End Notes

[1] In addition, the health reform legislation (P.L. 111-148) added a Medicare tax of 3.8% in 2013 and thereafter on some passive capital income, such as capital gains and dividends, for higher income taxpayers.

[2] For more details on the historical treatment of dividends, please see CRS Report RL3 1597, *The Taxation of Dividend Income: An Overview and Economic Analysis of the Issues*, by Jane G. Gravelle.

[3] As mentioned above, some passive income, including dividends, of higher income taxpayers would be subject to a Medicare tax of 3.8% beginning in 2013 under the health reform legislation (P.L. 111-148).

[4] For more information please see CRS Report R41362, *Who Doesn't Pay Income Taxes?*, by Thomas L. Hungerford.

[5] Even under an identical tax treatment, as was the case since 2003, capital gains might remain more advantageous from the tax perspective since taxpayers can select the timing of capital gains income in a manner minimizing their tax liability. In contrast, dividends are usually paid on a set schedule.

[6] Department of the Treasury, Internal Revenue Service, Form 1040 Instructions, 2005, p. 79. Similar tables in more recent years did not provide a necessary level of detail.

[7] U.S. Congress, Joint Committee on Taxation, *Estimated Budget Effects of the Revenue Provisions Contained in the President's Fiscal Year 2011 Budget Proposal*, JCX-7-10 R, 111th Cong., 2nd sess., March 15, 2010, p. 1.

[8] Department of the Treasury, General Explanations of the Administration's Fiscal Year 2011 Revenue Proposals ("Green Book"), February 2010, p. 131, available at http://www.treas.gov/offices/tax-policy/library/greenbk10.pdf.

[9] United States Senate, Budget Committee, Majority Staff, "Summary, Chairman's Mark FY20 11 Senate Budget Resolution," press release, April 21, 2010.

[10] Brett Ferguson and Jonathan Nicholson, "Lawmakers Ponder Senate Budget Resolution for Clues on Dividend Tax Rates," *Daily Tax Report*, 81 DTR G-1 1, April 29, 2010.

[11] Examples include H.R. 301, H.R. 470, H.R. 498, H.R. 664, H.R. 782, H.R. 4270, H.R. 4746, H.R. 5029, S. 567, S. 722, most of which propose indefinite extension of the JGTRRA tax treatment in various contexts. This is only a partial list.

[12] When analyzing this and subsequent tables, it is important to remember that the width of the AGI bands vary. For lower income classes the income bands typically span $10,000 (e.g., $20,000 to $30,000), but for the higher income classes they may be much wider (e.g., $2,000,000 to $5,000,000 spans $3,000,000). Obviously, increasing the width of an income band would increase the number of taxpayers in that band and the amount of the capital gains attributed to them.

[13] On occasion, the report refers to qualified dividends as "dividends" for brevity.

[14] This projection assumes reasonable growth of the dividend income between 2006 and 2012. In case of turmoil in the financial markets, similar to the one experienced in 2008, or lower economic growth, the impact may be lower. This report, however, focuses on the long run policy implications under normal circumstances, not on one-time events.

[15] The exact amount is highly sensitive to other possible changes to the tax system, but it would be substantial under most realistic scenarios. It would be much larger than the CBO estimate presented in the next item under identical assumptions about the future policies.

[16] Congressional Budget Office, *An Analysis of the President's Budgetary Proposals for Fiscal Year 2011,* March 2010, p. 18, available at http://cbo.gov/ftpdocs/112xx/doc11280/03-24-apb.pdf, or JCT, *Estimated Budget Effects of the Revenue Provisions Contained in the President's Fiscal Year 2011 Budget Proposal*, JCX-7-10 R.

INDEX

A

adjustment, 25
agencies, 28, 29, 33, 50
aggregation, 33
assets, vii, 1, 2, 4, 6, 7, 8, 12, 13, 15, 18, 19, 20, 24, 25, 26, 29, 30, 34, 35, 43, 50, 55, 56
avoidance, 2

B

benefits, vii, 1, 6, 7, 66, 70
bias, 34, 42
bonds, 18, 23, 55
budget deficit, 11, 14, 22, 71
budget resolution, 58
budget surplus, 22
businesses, 20

C

candidates, 4
cash, 34, 43
challenges, 42, 70
classes, 11, 12, 54, 55, 59, 60, 61, 62, 63, 73
complexity, 1, 8, 54, 68
conference, 4
confidentiality, 47
consumption, 13, 71
correlation, 16
cost, vii, 1, 3, 5, 7, 33, 49, 57, 58, 68
covering, 44
criticism, 1

D

data set, 42
deduction, 57
deficit, 11, 14, 22, 50
demand curve, 24
dependent variable, 50
depreciation, 2
derivatives, 46
disposable income, 71
distortions, 7
distribution, 19, 20, 21, 22, 25, 56, 58, 59, 61, 62, 63, 66

E

earnings, 2, 7
economies of scale, 25
election, 4
emergency, 70
endogeneity, 42
endowments, 23
entrepreneurs, 8
entrepreneurship, 7, 8

environment, 70
equity, 7, 8
evidence, 5, 7, 8, 12, 16, 17, 23, 26, 28, 35, 37, 39, 42, 45, 49
exclusion, vii, 1, 2, 3, 4, 5, 9, 12, 31, 37, 46

F

families, 20, 23, 25
financial, 18, 23, 46, 73
fiscal policy, 71
fixed rate, 31
flaws, 34
fluctuations, 31, 58
formula, 38
foundations, 23
funds, 8, 18, 19, 20, 23

G

goods and services, 24
greed, 4
gross domestic product, 15
growth, 1, 6, 7, 12, 22, 24, 73
guidance, 28

H

health, 32, 72, 73
history, 8, 11, 12, 14
homes, 8, 18, 19
horizontal equity, 8
household income, 25
housing, 2, 4, 7
human, 23

I

identification, 45
indexing, 4, 8, 9
inertia, 23
inflation, 2, 3, 4, 6, 8, 13
issues, 18, 32, 36, 47, 49, 50, 57
itemized deductions, 56

L

lead, 8, 17, 37, 46
legislation, vii, 1, 12, 31, 32, 50, 72, 73
lifetime, 3
livestock, 55
lock-in effects, 15
long-term gains, 1

M

magnitude, vii, 1, 6, 24, 30, 35, 37, 45
majority, 54, 59, 60, 62
married couples, 27, 29
methodology, 33, 39, 43, 46

N

neutral, 17, 69

O

opportunities, 15
ownership, 20

P

parity, 54, 57, 68
penalties, 6
portfolio, 37, 50
preferential treatment, 11, 12, 56
preparation, 68
project, 35
public assistance, 20, 25

R

rate of return, 6, 7, 23
recession, 49
reconciliation, 4

reform, 1, 3, 26, 31, 47, 50, 72, 73
regression, 36, 42, 43, 44, 45, 46, 47, 50
relief, 8, 58, 68, 71
researchers, 42, 50
resolution, 58
response, 5, 6, 7, 16, 17, 28, 29, 30, 31, 33, 34, 35, 37, 38, 39, 41, 46, 50
restrictions, 70
retirement, 7, 18, 56, 69
revenue, 3, 5, 7, 11, 14, 15, 16, 17, 26, 27, 28, 29, 30, 31, 32, 33, 34, 35, 38, 39, 40, 49, 50, 58, 68, 69, 71
risk, 23
root, 25
rules, 2, 7, 23, 57

S

savings, 5, 6, 7, 70
scope, 35
self-control, 23
sensitivity, 26
services, 24
shareholders, vii, 53, 56
shock, 49
simulation, 17
solution, 71
specifications, 17, 43, 46, 47, 50
spending, 24
state, 36, 37, 45, 46, 49
states, 25, 45
statistics, 65
stimulus, 4, 12, 22, 24, 71
stock, 2, 4, 6, 7, 8, 12, 16, 24, 31, 39, 49, 56
structure, 54, 55, 56, 57, 64, 67, 68, 69, 70
substitution, 6, 23
supply curve, 24
surplus, 22

T

target, 1, 23
techniques, 28, 42, 45
time periods, 43
time series, 33, 34, 35, 37, 39, 42, 46, 51
total revenue, 32, 49
transactions, 36, 42
treatment, vii, viii, 2, 3, 4, 8, 11, 12, 49, 50, 53, 54, 55, 56, 57, 64, 65, 67, 68, 72, 73

V

variables, 33, 35, 40, 42, 44, 46, 50, 58
variations, 45
vein, 58
venture capital, 8, 23

W

wages, vii, 53
wealth, 13, 23, 25, 26

Y

yield, 70